WORDS
OF WAR

For
My Mother
Alice, Oonagh and Lucinda

WORDS OF WAR

SPEECHES THAT INSPIRED HEROIC DEEDS

Anthony Weldon

BENE FACTUM PUBLISHING

Words of War

Published in 2012 by
Bene Factum Publishing Ltd
PO Box 58122
London
SW8 5WZ
Email: inquiries@bene-factum.co.uk
www.bene-factum.co.uk

ISBN: 978-1-903071-63-2

A CIP catalogue record of this is available from the British Library

Cover design and typesetting: Ian Hughes – Mousemat Design Limited
Printed in Malta for Latitude Press

Contents

PREFACE

It would seem that the day of the set-piece conventional battle is over. For centuries their format changed little – with opposing troops lined up facing each other and often with their leaders to the fore – be they monarchs or generals – exhorting their side to fight for their cause's greater good.

Even if this scenario has now changed, the need for leaders to communicate in times of adversity has not. While compiling this book a number of themes common to all periods and types of warfare have emerged – inspiring words encouraging incredible courage, even when the odds look overwhelming, have resulted in acts of almost unbelievable bravery, the necessity to convey the right of a cause to ensure that there is no breakdown of morale on the battlefield nor on the home front, and the requirement for underlying codes of duty and honour to make men fight to win.

For 'Words of War' I have drawn on many sources. Some periods of history have been much more fruitful than others – often for the practical reason that at the time there were more reliable methods of recording speeches exactly. The American Civil War and also World War II have provided particularly rich pickings.

What I have found absolutely fascinating are the different speaking styles and content of military and political leaders – for example two of World War II's great generals. Field Marshal Montgomery was succinct and very British whilst US General George Patton had panache and a direct style all of his own. Despite these contrasts each was equally effective in inspiring their own troops on to victory.

Most absorbing of all are the extraordinary differences, and also some of the similarities it has to be said, between the British Prime Minister Winston Churchill's and the German leader Adolf Hitler's oratorical styles. Both spoke at length with mesmerising content to their parliaments but with wider audiences in mind. What comes through are Churchill's great oratorical dignity in the face of adversity against Hitler's megalomania and aspiration to conquer the world. I found this particular aspect of my research completely absorbing.

In some cases I have quoted complete speeches and in other incidences I have edited considerably as I best saw fit to convey what the speaker was trying to say under the circumstances prevalent at the time of his or her words. These editorial decisions are mine alone. For example both Churchill's and Hitler's speeches were very long – too long for an anthology such as this. What to cut out and what to keep were very difficult decisions. I hope the result is that I have succeeded in giving the reader the reason why such words had the impact and significance they did.

I have also interspersed the substantially longer speeches with very brief quotes, insightful one-liners and on occasions a light-hearted look at conflict. Every so often I have veered away from the spoken word to include writing and thoughts about war and adversity. I have even included a Declaration of War (Hitler's against America) which isn't a speech but I feel is worth reading in the context of this book.

I hope that all the entries in this book throw some light onto the words that drive heroic deeds in the face of adversity.

In my endeavours I have been assisted with advice, welcome critical comments and additional research by Prue Fox, Tom Guest, Dominic Horsfall, Alex Martin, Donough O'Brien and Eleanor Wilkinson – to them my thanks and appreciation.

Anthony Weldon
London 2012

DEFIANCE AGAINST ALL ODDS

"Defeat—I do not recognise the meaning of the word!"

Margaret Thatcher

Dieneces

In 480BC the invading Persians under Xerxes reached the Pass at Thermopylae where 300 Greeks fought an epic rearguard action to allow the remainder of their army to escape. At one point the sky was so darkened by such a vast number of Persian arrows that Spartan Dieneces joked:

"Our friend brings us good news. If the Persians darken the sun with their arrows, we will be able to fight in the shade."

Hannibal

Latin proverb, most commonly attributed to Hannibal in response to his generals who had declared it impossible to cross the Alps with elephants in 218BC:

"Aut viam inveniam aut faciam."
(*"I will either find a way, or make one."*)

Elazar Ben-Yair

In AD 66, having withstood three months besieged at Masada by the Romans, and facing a certain defeat the following day, Elazar Ben-Yair gathered his people together before their mass suicide and addressed them:

"Since we long ago resolved never to be servants to the Romans, nor to any other than to God Himself, Who alone is the true and just Lord of mankind, the time is now come that obliges us to make that resolution true in practice...We were the very first that revolted, and we are the last to fight against them; and I cannot but esteem it as a favour that God has granted us, that it is still in our power to die bravely, and in a state of freedom.

In our case it is evident that day-break will end our resistance, but we are free to choose an honourable death with our loved ones...Let our wives die unabused, our children without knowledge of slavery. After that, let us do each other an ungrudging kindness, preserving our freedom as a glorious winding-sheet. But first, let our possessions and the whole fortress go up in flames. It will be a bitter blow to the Romans, that I know, to find our persons beyond their reach and nothing left for them to loot.

One thing only let us spare – our store of food: it will bear witness when we are dead to the fact that we perished, not through want but because, as we resolved at the beginning, we chose death rather than slavery... Come! While our hands are free and can hold a sword, let them do a noble service! Let us die unenslaved by our enemies, and leave this world as free men in company with our wives and children."

Joan of Arc

The French heroine, also known as the 'Maid of Orléans', came from a humble background to become the iconic leader of the French army in the Hundred Years War (1337-1453). This is her letter, written in 1429, to the King of England, Henry VI, who was besieging Orléans:

"King of England, render account to the King of Heaven of your royal blood. Return the keys of all the good cities which you have seized, to the Maid. She is sent by God to reclaim the royal blood, and is fully prepared to make peace, if you will give her satisfaction; that is, you must render justice, and pay back all that you have taken.

King of England, if you do not do these things, I am the commander of the military; and in whatever place I shall find your men in France, I will make them flee the country, whether they wish to or not; and if they will not obey, the Maid will have them all killed. She comes sent by the King of Heaven, body for body, to take you out of France, and the Maid promises and certifies to you that if you do not leave France she and her troops will raise a mighty outcry as has not been heard in France in a thousand years. And believe that the King of Heaven has sent her so much power that you will not be able to harm her or her brave army.

To you, archers, noble companions in arms, and all people who are before Orléans, I say to you in God's name, go home to your own country; if you do not do so, beware of the Maid, and of the damages you will suffer. Do not attempt to remain, for you have no rights in France from God, the King of Heaven, and the Son of the Virgin Mary. It is Charles, the rightful heir, to whom God has given France, who will shortly enter Paris in a grand company. If you do not believe the news written of God and the Maid, then in whatever place we may find you, we will soon see who has the better right, God or you.

William de la Pole, Count of Suffolk, Sir John Talbot, and Thomas, Lord Scales, lieutenants of the Duke of Bedford, who calls himself regent of the King of France for the King of England, make a response, if you wish to make peace over the city of Orleans! If you do not do so, you will always recall the damages which will attend you.

Duke of Bedford, who call yourself regent of France for the King of England, the Maid asks you not to make her destroy you. If you do not render her satisfaction, she and the French will perform the greatest feat ever, in the name of Christianity.

Done on the Tuesday of Holy Week (March 22, 1429). Hear the words of God and the Maid."

Sir Francis Drake

Speech to his crew off of Puerto San Julian, Argentina, prior to entering the stormy Strait of Magellan (May 1578):

"For by the life of God, it doth even take my wits from me to think on it. Here is such controversy between the sailors and gentlemen, and such stomaching between the gentlemen and sailors, it doth make me mad to hear it. But, my masters, I must have it left. For I must have the gentleman to haul and draw with the mariner, and the mariner with the gentleman. What! let us show ourselves to be of a company and let us not give occasion to the enemy to rejoice at our decay and overthrow. I would know him that would refuse to set his hand to a rope, but I know there is not any such here..."

John Paul Jones

At the Battle of Flamborough Head in March 1779,
Commanding the USS Bonhomme Richard, *John Paul Jones*
decided to attack a British merchant convoy, and engaged an
escort vessel, HMS Serapis, *led by Captain Richard Pearson. At*
the height of the battle, John Paul Jones was prematurely asked
to surrender. This was his reply:

"I have not yet begun to fight."

Duke of Wellington

Battle of Waterloo 1815:

"Hard pounding this, Gentlemen.
Let's see who will pound the longest".

William B. Travis

In 1836 American settlers in Texas demanded to be
independent from Mexico and eventually rebelled. 188 Texans
and American frontiersmen (including Jim Bowie and Davy
Crockett) were besieged for twelve days by a vastly superior
Mexican force in the Alamo in San Antonio. On 24 February,
Travis sent out the following message:

"To the people of Texas and all Americans in the world:
Fellow citizens and compatriots – I am besieged, by a thousand
or more of the Mexicans under Santa Anna – I have sustained a
continual bombardment and cannonade for 24 hours and have

not lost a man – The enemy has demanded a surrender at discretion, otherwise, the garrison are to be put to the sword, if the fort is taken – I have answered the demand with a cannon shot, and our flag still waves proudly from the walls – I shall never surrender or retreat. Then, I call on you in the name of Liberty, of patriotism and everything dear to the American character, to come to our aid, with all dispatch – The enemy is receiving reinforcements daily and will no doubt increase to three or four thousand in four or five days. If this call is neglected, I am determined to sustain myself as long as possible and die like a soldier who never forgets what is due to his own honor and that of his country – VICTORY OR DEATH.

Lt. Col. comdt.

P.S. The Lord is on our side – When the enemy appeared in sight we had not three bushels of corn –We have since found in deserted houses 80 or 90 bushels and got into the walls 20 or 30 head of Beeves."

Commander William Travis refused offers of surrender and addressed the defenders on 5 March:

"My choice is to stay in this fort and die for my country, fighting as long as breath should remain in my body. This I will do even if you leave me alone. Do as you think best, but no man can die with me without affording me comfort at the moment of my death."

In the final assault every defender died but at the cost of 1500 Mexican soldiers killed.

Giuseppe Garibaldi

Rome, July 2, 1849

"Soldiers, I am going out from Rome. Let those who wish to continue the war against the stranger, come with me. I offer neither pay, nor quarters, nor provisions. I offer hunger, thirst, forced marches, battles, and death. Let him who loves his country follow me."

Marshal of France Patrice MacMahon

In 1854, during the Crimean War, MacMahon commanded French troops at the long drawn-out Siege of Sevastopol and was advised to give up after a year. His retort is now famous:

"J'y suis. J'y reste!"
(*"I'm here. I'm staying here!"*)

MacMahon's persistence and the eventual French assault on key Russian redoubts led to the fall of Sevastopol for the Allies and the end of the Crimean War.

Captain Danjou, Second Lieutenant Maudet and Legionnaire Berg

Whilst beating off assault after assault by Colonel Milan's Juarist Mexican cavalry, holed up in the little hamlet of Camarón in 1863, Foreign Legion Captain Danjou with 64 Legionnaires resisted Milan's demands to surrender, saying:

"We have munitions, we will not surrender."

Danjou died of wounds, and Second Lieutenant Maudet took command. The survivors held off the attack of 2,000 Mexican soldiers for ten hours. When out of ammunition Maudet and the last five Legionnaires charged the enemy – one was killed instantly and two were wounded. The surviving three were surrounded and asked to surrender and Maine replied

"On the condition we keep our weapons and you look after our officer"

"To men such as you, one refuses nothing"
was the Mexican officer's response.

Later when the three were bought before the Mexican commander he could not believe that they were the only survivors and remarked

"Truly these are not men, but demons"

Legionnaire Berg received permission to write a report to his Legion Commanding officer which read

"The Third Company of the 1st is dead, my Colonel, but it did enough to make those who speak of it say 'It had nothing but good soldiers.' "

This epic action is still commemorated by the French Foreign Legionnaire on 30th April each year.

General Thomas "Stonewall" Jackson

American Civil War Confederate general

"Don't say it's impossible! Turn your command over to the next officer. If he can't do it, I'll find someone who can, even if I have to take him from the ranks!"

Colonel Joshua Lawrence Chamberlain

Little Round Top hill was the key feature on the Gettysburg battlefield (July 1863) in the American Civil War. In the decisive moment the Union forces under Chamberlain's orders were to hold 'at all hazards' and so, despite being seriously outflanked, he decided to charge:

"Not a moment was about to be lost! Five minutes more of such a defensive and the last roll call would sound for us" Desperate as the chances were, there was nothing for it but to take the offensive. I stepped to the colours. The men turned towards me. One word was enough – 'BAYONETS!' It caught like fire and swept along the ranks."

Stepan O. Makarov

Imperial Russian Navy Admiral, 1863–1904

"My rule is: If you meet the weakest vessel, attack. If it is a vessel equal to yours, attack. And if it is stronger than yours, also attack."

Grand Duke Nicholas of Russia

In 1877, Tsar Alexander II attacked the Ottoman Empire, designating his brother Grand Duke Nicholas to lead the Russian army of 150,000. At Plevna, a tiny force of Turks, headed by Osman Pasha, held back the huge Russian army for over 5 months. When finally forced to surrender by sheer numbers of soldiers, the wounded Osman was told by Grand Duke Nicholas:

"I congratulate you on your success in defending Plevna. This is one of the most splendid exploits in history."

David Lloyd George

On the outbreak of WWI – London, 19 September, 1914

"They think we cannot beat them. It will not be easy. It will be a long job; it will be a terrible war; but in the end we shall march through terror to triumph."

General Ferdinand Foch

French General Ferdinand Foch to General Joffre during WWI Battle of the Marne 1914

"Hard pressed on my right; my left is in retreat. My centre is yielding. Impossible to manoeuvre. Situation excellent. I am attacking. Attaquez!"

Major Gavrilovic

Speech to the Serbian Infantry 1915

"At three o'clock sharp, the enemy must be crushed by your mighty charge, torn to pieces by your grenades and bayonets. The honour of our Serbian capital Belgrade must be spotless. Soldiers, heroes, The Supreme Command has erased our names from its roll. Our regiment is sacrificed for our King and Fatherland. You don't have to worry anymore about your lives that no longer exist. So forward, to glory! Long live Serbia! Long live the King! Long live Belgrade!"

A few hours later, 233 soldiers of the 340 member-strong volunteer unit were dead. Major Gavrilovic was himself badly wounded. But he survived to fight again, as commander of the 1st battalion of the victorious 12th Serbian infantry division at the Thessalonica (Greece) front in 1918. The gallant sacrifice of the 233 Belgrade volunteers in 1915 gave the bulk of the Serbian army enough time to retreat, regroup and eventually win the war

Alvin York

A famous American World War I crack shot and hero, York was born in Fentress County, Tennessee, and drafted into the U. S. Army in 1917. The next year, in the Battle of the Argonne Forest, as one of only eight men left in action, he reportedly killed 25 Germans and captured 132 prisoners. His account of the scene was thus:

"Those machine guns were spitting fire and cutting down the undergrowth all around me something awful. And the Germans were yelling orders. You never heard such a racket in all your life. I didn't have time to dodge behind a tree or dive into the brush...As soon as the machine guns opened fire on me, I began to exchange shots with them. There were over 30 of them in continuous action, and all I could do was touch the Germans off just as fast as I could. I was sharp shooting . . . all the time I kept yelling at them to come down. I didn't want to kill any more than I had to. But it was they or I. And I was giving them the best I had."

Then asked by an incredulous officer how many German prisoners he and the remaining men had taken, York replied:

"Hell, Lieutenant, I ain't had time to count them."

Admiral of the Fleet Andrew Cunningham

British Commander-in-Chief of the Mediterranean Fleet – before attacking the Italian fleet at Taranto – 11 November 1940:

"We are outnumbered, there is only one thing to do.
We must attack!"

Kenneth Taylor

At Pearl Harbour, Hawaii, on the morning of Sunday 7th December 1941, Second Lieutenants George Welch and Kenneth Taylor were just about to have a final nightcap after an all night party, when they surveyed with horror the scene of devastation developing before them on the airstrip, caused by a surprise attack by the Japanese Imperial Navy. Luckily, their planes were parked on a grass airstrip 10 miles away at Haleiwa. Defying senior authority, Taylor phoned the airfield and shouted:

"Get two P-40s ready. No, it's not a gag – the Japs are here!"

They were just two of a handful of pilots who were able to get into the air in an attempt to fight back against the overwhelming force of 350 Japanese aircraft.

General Douglas MacArthur

Douglas MacArthur was an American general (and also field marshal of the Philippine army) who was Chief of Staff of the United States Army during the 1930s.

"Age wrinkles the body. Quitting wrinkles the soul."

Ho Chi Minh

Communist leader of the Vietnamese battle for independence in the 1950s and 1960s

"You fools! Don't you realize what it means if the Chinese remain? Don't you remember your history? The last time the Chinese came, they stayed a thousand years. The French are foreigners. They are weak. Colonialism is dying. The white man is finished in Asia. But if the Chinese stay now, they will never go. As for me, I prefer to sniff French shit for five years than to eat Chinese shit for the rest of my life."

British Prime Minister Margaret Thatcher

This was Prime Minister Thatcher's response when, prior to the 1982 Falklands War, she was told that engaging Britain in such a seemingly irrelevant conflict thousands of miles from Europe could result in defeat.

"Defeat—I do not recognise the meaning of the word!"

THE FOOLHARDY and THE HUMOROUS IN THE FACE OF ADVERSITY

"The pessimist sees difficulty in every opportunity. The optimist sees opportunity in every difficulty."

Winston Churchill

King Gustavus Adolphus of Sweden

Before the Battle of Lützen (1632) the Swedish King Gustavus Adolphus, one of Europe's greatest military leaders, declined to wear his armour – not for any vainglorious reason but because he had been wounded in a previous battle. He died at Lützen leading a cavalry charge.

"The Lord God is my Armour"

Lord North

The British Prime Minister (1770–1782), Lord North, underestimated the gravity of the situation on the 1774 declaration of the American War of Independence which ultimately led to America ceasing to be a British colony:

"Four or five frigates will do the business without any military force."

Duke of Wellington

Arthur Wellesley is considered one of Britain's greatest generals and rose to prominence during the Napoleonic Wars. He was created Duke of Wellington in 1814 and was the victor of the Battle of Waterloo in June 1815 when he remarked about his own troops:

"I don't know what effect the men will have on the enemy, but, by god they frighten me."

General Lord Raglan

Commander British troops Crimea 1854. This miscommunicated order meant the British Light Brigade disastrously charged the wrong Russian guns at the Battle of Balaclava.

"Lord Raglan wishes the Cavalry to advance rapidly to the front, follow the enemy, and try to prevent the enemy carrying away the guns. Troop Horse Artillery may accompany. French Cavalry is on your left. Immediate."

Alfred Lord Tennyson's epic poem captures both the glory as well as the futility of this famous incident:

Half a league, half a league,
Half a league onward,
All in the valley of Death
Rode the six hundred.
"Forward, the Light Brigade!
Charge the guns!" he said:
Into the valley of Death
Rode the six hundred.

William Tecumseh Sherman

Union general – American Civil War (1861–1865)

"Grant stood by me when I was crazy, and I stood by him when he was drunk, and now we stand by each other."

"If I had my choice I would kill every reporter in the world, but I am sure we would be getting reports from Hell before breakfast."

"I think I understand what military fame is; to be killed on the field of battle and have your name misspelled in the newspapers."

General Thomas "Stonewall" Jackson

Confederate General – American Civil War

"When war does come, my advice is to draw the sword and throw away the scabbard."

Colonel Joshua Lawrence Chamberlain

Battle of Gettysburg 1863, as Union troops rushed to fill the gap in the battlefield, Chamberlain sent his two brothers to different parts of the line to lessen the risk of them all being killed together, saying:

"Boys, another shot might make it difficult for mother."

Robert E. Lee

American Civil War commander of the Confederate Army of North Virginia:

"I like whiskey. I always did, and that is why I never drink it."

General George Custer

In 1876 the North American native Sioux tribes led by Chiefs Crazy Horse and Sitting Bull refused to be contained in their reservations. Lieutenant General George Custer and his 7th Cavalry were sent to pursue them. When he discovered the Indian camp at the Little Big Horn River, Custer unwisely split his forces. He and 211 men charged in towards the centre of the camp and was surprised by an overwhelming Indian attack. Everyone of his force was killed, including two of his brothers who were serving with him, so Custer's last words before he charged are without verification, but are thought to be:

"Hurrah boys, we've got them. We'll finish them up and go home to the station".

His last recorded words, a few hours earlier, were:

"Custer's luck! The biggest Indian village on the Continent."

Robert Baden-Powell

In 1899 during South Africa's Second Boer War, the Boers laid siege to Mafeking. Garrison commander Colonel Baden-Powell organised such diversions as concerts and cricket matches to boost his British troops' morale. The young Boer commander Sarel Eloff, a grandson of President Kruger, became so bored and frustrated watching that he sent Baden-Powell a message:

"To Colonel Baden-Powell, I see in the Bulawayo Chronicle that your men in Mafeking play cricket on Sundays and give concerts and balls on Sunday evenings. In case you would allow my men to join in the same, it would be very agreeable to me; as here outside Mafeking there are seldom any of the fair sex and there can be no merriment without their being present...
Wishing you a pleasant day. I remain your obliging friend, S. Eloff, Commandant of Johannesburg."

To which Robert Baden-Powell replied:

"Sir, I beg to thank you for your letter of yesterday... I should like nothing better – after the match in which we are at present engaged is over. But just now we are having our innings and have so far scored 180 days, not out, against the bowling of Cronje, Snijmna, Botha...and we are having a very enjoyable game.
I remain yours truly,
R.S.S. Baden-Powell"

General Gerard Leman

In August 1914, during the defence of Liège, Leman continued to fight despite having had both legs crushed, and when the town was finally overrun, he was carried out, unconscious, on a stretcher by his orderlies. To their German vanquishers the medical orderlies said:

"Please respect the General, he is dead."

But Leman had regained consciousness and replied:

"It is as it is. Please put in your dispatches that I was unconscious."

Albert Jacka

In May 1915, fighting the Turks at Gallipoli, Australian Imperial Forces volunteer 'Bert' Jacka charged the enemy line and captured their trench singlehandedly. He was found by his unit the following dawn, surrounded by bodies, with an unlit cigarette in his mouth. He told Lieutenant Crabbe:

"Well, I got the beggars, Sir!"

Jacka was the first Australian to receive the Victoria Cross.

Lt. Colonel Sir John Milbanke, Bt. VC

Commanding The Sherwood Rangers – Gallipoli, August 1915:

"I don't know where it is, and don't think anybody else does either, but in any case we are to go ahead and attack any Turks we meet."

Kaiser Wilhelm II

The German Emperor on commencement of the Serbian Campaign in 1915:

"Heroes, I am sending you to a new war against a small, but very brave nation. They are the Serbs, who, during three consecutive wars – against Turkey, Bulgaria and Austria-Hungary – proved to the world that they possess the finest warrior qualities and the greatest military abilities and who, on blood-splattered flags, have written only the greatest and the most glorious victories during the past four years. You must be aware that only your energy and readiness for the greatest sacrifices and only complete disdain for death will enable you to conquer this nation and their country and bring a new victory to the German army. May victory and glory be ours! Hooray!"

Having been informed that Bulgaria had capitulated and signed an armistice agreement in September 1918, the German Kaiser, Wilhelm II, sent a telegram full of bitterness to his ally in World War I, the Austro-Hungarian Emperor:

"62,000 Serbs have decided the outcome of this war. Shame on us!"

Prime Minister Neville Chamberlain

Speaking from 10 Downing Street on the 30th September 1938 after Chamberlain returned from meeting Germany's Chancellor Adolf Hitler to sign the Munich Agreement in an attempt to prevent the outbreak of WWII:

"My good friends, this is the second time in our history that there has come back from Germany to Downing Street peace with honour. I believe it is peace for our time. Go home and get a nice, quiet sleep."

That day's Daily Express front page headline:

"Britain will not be involved in a European war this year, or next year either."

Reichsmarschall Hermann Goering

1939 – just before the outbreak of WWII and the eventual Allied bombing campaign against Germany:

"The Ruhr will not be subject to a single bomb. If an enemy reaches the Ruhr, my name is not Herman Goering; you can call me Meier."

US Duty Officer Kermit Tyler

At 7.02 am on Sunday 7th December 1941, two US radar operators on the early warning system at Opana Point, Hawaii were about to turn off their radar set when they picked up a "blip" denoting at least 50 planes approaching. They reported this to the tired and ill-informed duty officer Kermit Tyler (he had never seen a radar set) who assumed this "blip" to be a small in-coming flight of American B-17 bombers due in from San Francisco. He dismissed the report with:

"Well don't worry about it"

The blip was in fact the first wave of 350 incoming Japanese planes which started the surprise attack on Pearl Harbour and resulted in the USA joining World War II.

General Norman 'Dutch' Cota

Omaha Beach, Normandy 1944:

"Gentlemen, we are being killed on the beaches. Let's go inland and be killed."

General George Patton

American General who made his name successfully commanding US troops in North Africa and Europe during World War II

On leadership:

"A piece of spaghetti or a military unit can only be led from the front end."

Directing his reconnaissance troops:

"Just drive down that road until you get blown up."

General McAuliffe

The single word reply in 1944 by McAuliffe, the US General commanding the 101st Airborne Division, to the ultimatum to surrender offered by the Germans surrounding Bastogne, Belgium. Not surprisingly The Germans were perplexed by the answer, but the 101st managed to hold out until relieved.

"Nuts!"

Col. William O. Darby

US Rangers – World War II

"Onward we stagger, and if the tanks come, may God help the tanks."

General Oliver P. Smith

Smith was a U.S. Marine Corps General and a highly decorated combat veteran of World War II and then the Korean War. During the Battle of Chosin Reservoir (1950), when his troops, the 1st Marine Division, performed a tactical retreat, he said:

"We are not retreating—we are advancing in another direction."

Field Marshal Viscount Slim

WWII Commander of the 14th "Forgotten" Army in Burma

"War is God's way of teaching Americans geography."

US Admiral Leahy

Reporting to newly appointed President Truman on the development of the Atomic bomb which, was subsequently dropped in 1945 on Hiroshima (6th August) and Nagasaki (9th August) causing enormous death tolls and brought the war to an early end:

"The atomic bomb will never go off, and I speak as an expert in explosives."

Fidel Castro

Cuban dictator (1959-2008) – commenting on his distinctive beard

"The story of our beards is very simple, it arose out of the difficult conditions we were living and fighting under as guerrillas. We didn't have any razor blades so everybody let their beards and hair grow, and that turned into a kind of badge of identity. For the campesinos and everybody else, for the press, for the reporters, we were "los barbudos". It had a positive side: in order for a spy to infiltrate us, he had to start months ahead of time – he'd have to have six months growth of beard…Later with the triumph of the Revolution we kept our beards to preserve the symbolism."

Colonel Chargin' Charlie Beckwith

Founder of the US special operations Delta Force

"We ain't making no goddamn cornflakes here."

Saddam Hussein

Mother of all battles – 17th Jan 1991

"The great duel, the mother of all battles has begun… The dawn of victory nears as this great showdown begins!"

General "Stormin' Norman" Schwarzkopf

Commander Coalition Forces – Gulf War 1991

"As far as Saddam Hussein being a great military strategist, he is neither a strategist, nor is he schooled in the operational arts, nor is he a tactician, nor is he a general, nor is he a soldier. Other than that, he's a great military man, I want you to know that."

On life after retirement

"A couple of years ago I told 541,000 men what to do and when to do and it was done! Now I can't get a plumber to come to the house."

Whitney Brown

American comedian commenting on the first Gulf War (1990–1991)

"Our bombs are smarter than the average high school student. At least they can find Kuwait."

"Hit the other fellow, as quick as you can, and as hard as you can, where it hurts him most, when he ain't lookin'."

US Marine saying

"Nobody ever drowned in sweat."

Donald Rumsfeld

In 2002 the United States Government was determinedly trying to prove the existence of Iraq's weapons of mass destruction. Secretary of Defence Donald Rumsfeld summed up the availability of hard information in a way that we "all know what he means" even though it sounds wonderfully nonsensical:

"There are known knowns. These are things we know that we know. There are known unknowns. That is to say, there are things that we know we don't know. But there are also unknown unknowns. There are things we don't know we don't know."

George W Bush

American President (2001–20090)

"I'm telling you there's an enemy that would like to attack America, Americans, again. There just is. That's the reality of the world. And I wish him all the very best."

LEADING FROM THE FRONT

INSPIRATIONAL MILITARY LEADERS

"A leader is a dealer in hope."

Napoleon Bonaparte

Queen Elizabeth 1

At Tilbury, England, August 1588, to troops assembled to repel the Spanish Armada:

"My loving people,
We have been persuaded by some that are careful of our safety, to take heed how we commit ourselves to armed multitudes, for fear of treachery; but I assure you I do not desire to live to distrust my faithful and loving people. Let tyrants fear, I have always so behaved myself that, under God, I have placed my chiefest strength and safeguard in the loyal hearts and good-will of my subjects; and therefore I am come amongst you, as you see, at this time, not for my recreation and disport, but being resolved, in the midst and heat of the battle, to live and die amongst you all; to lay down for my God, and for my kingdom, and my people, my honour and my blood, even in the dust. I know I have the body but of a weak and feeble woman; but I have the heart and stomach of a king, and of a king of England too, and think foul scorn that Parma or Spain, or any prince of Europe, should dare to invade the borders of my realm; to which rather than any dishonour shall grow by me, I myself will take up arms, I myself will be your general, judge, and rewarder of every one of your virtues in the field. I know already, for your forwardness you have deserved rewards and crowns; and We do assure you in the word of a prince, they shall be duly paid you. In the mean time, my lieutenant general shall be in my stead, than whom never prince commanded a more noble or worthy subject; not doubting but by your obedience to my general, by your concord in the camp, and your valour in the field, we shall shortly have a famous victory over those enemies of my God, of my kingdom, and of my people."

George Washington

Founding father of the United States and Commander-in-Chief of the American troops in the War of Independence (1775–1783) against the British.

General Orders, Headquarters, New York (2 July 1776)

"Let us therefore animate and encourage each other, and show the whole world that a Freeman, contending for liberty on his own ground, is superior to any slavish mercenary on earth."

General Order, (9 July 1776)

"The General hopes and trusts that every officer and man will endeavor to live and act as becomes a Christian soldier defending the dearest rights and liberties of his country."

Address to the Continental Army before the Battle of Long Island (27 August 1776)

"The time is now near at hand which must probably determine whether Americans are to be freemen or slaves; whether they are to have any property they can call their own; whether their houses and farms are to be pillaged and destroyed, and themselves consigned to a state of wretchedness from which no human efforts will deliver them. The fate of unborn millions will now depend, under God, on the courage and conduct of this army. Our cruel and unrelenting enemy leaves us only the choice of brave resistance, or the most abject submission. We have, therefore, to resolve to conquer or die."

Encouraging his men to re-enlist in the army (31 December 1776)

"My brave fellows, you have done all I asked you to do, and more than can be reasonably expected; but your country is at stake, your wives, your houses and all that you hold dear. You have worn yourselves out with fatigues and hardships, but we know not how to spare you. If you will consent to stay one month longer, you will render that service to the cause of liberty, and to your country, which you probably can never do under any other circumstances."

Rallying his troops at the Battle of Princeton (3 January 1777)

"Parade with me my brave fellows, we will have them soon!"

Napoleon Bonaparte

In 1796, Napoleon, then a young officer of 27 years of age, was given command of the French army in Italy. In the Italian campaign, he demonstrated his genius for propaganda and psychological warfare, as the following selection of speeches to his troops makes clear.

At the beginning of the Italian Campaign [March 27, 1796] he addressed his army:

"Soldiers, you are naked, ill fed! The Government owes you much; it can give you nothing. Your patience, the courage you display in the midst of these rocks, are admirable; but they procure you no glory, no fame is reflected upon you. I seek to lead you into the most fertile plains in the world. Rich provinces, great cities will be in your power. There you will find honour, glory, and riches. Soldiers of Italy, would you be lacking in courage or constancy?"

Part of his subsequent Proclamation to the army [April 26, 1796]:

"In a fortnight you have won six victories, taken twenty-one standards, fifty-five pieces of cannon and several fortresses, overrun the richest part of Piedmont, you have made 15,000 prisoners and killed or wounded more than 10,000 men...

You have won battles without cannon, crossed rivers without bridges, made forced marches without shoes, camped without brandy and often without bread... Soldiers of liberty, only republican phalanxes could have endured what you have endured. Soldiers, you have our thanks! The grateful Patrie will owe its prosperity to you...

The two armies which but recently attacked you with audacity are fleeing before you in terror; the wicked men who laughed at your misery and rejoiced at the thought of the triumphs of your enemies are confounded and trembling...

Friends, I promise you this conquest; but there is one condition you must swear to fulfil —to respect the people whom you liberate, to repress the horrible pillaging committed by scoundrels incited by our enemies. Otherwise you would not be the liberators of the people; you would be their scourge...

But, soldiers, as yet you have done nothing compared with what remains to be done..."

In 1798 Napoleon invaded Egypt to strengthen the French presence in the Eastern Mediterranean and to threaten British power in India:

"Soldiers, you are a wing of the army of England! You have made war in the mountains, plains and cities. Naval war remains to complete your experience.

The Roman legions whom you have sometimes imitated, but not as yet equalled, fought Carthage successively upon this sea and upon the plains of Zama. Victory never forsook them, because they were constantly brave, patient of fatigue, well disciplined, resolute. But, soldiers, Europe has her eyes upon you! You have great destinies to fulfil, battles to fight, fatigues to surmount!

Frenchmen, you are about to undertake a conquest of which the effects upon the civilization and commerce of the world are incalculable. The first city you are to meet was founded by Alexander.

Cadis, Sheiks, Imams, Chorbadgys, you will be told that I came to destroy your religion; do not believe it. Let your answer be that I come to reestablish your rights and punish your usurpers, and that I have more respect than the Mamelukes for your god, his prophet, and the Koran.

Tell your people that all men are equal before God. Wisdom, talent, and virtue make the only difference between them. But, is there a fine country? It is appropriated by the Mamelukes. Is there a beautiful slave, a fine horse, a fine house? All this belongs to the Mamelukes. If Egypt be their farm, let them show the lease which God has given them of it! But God is just and merciful to the people. The Egyptians will be called to fill the public stations. Let the wisest, the most enlightened, the most virtuous govern, and the people will be happy.

You had formerly large cities, great canals, a flourishing commerce. What has ruined them all if not the avarice, the injustice, and the tyranny of the Mamelukes?

Cadis, Sheiks, Imams, Chorbadgys, tell the people that we, too, are true Mussulmans. Is it not we who demolished the Pope, the great enemy of the Mussulmans? Are we not the friends of the grand seigneur?

Thrice happy those who shall be found on our side! They will prosper in fortune and rank. Happy those who shall remain neutral! They will have time to know the result, and then will join us.

But woe, eternal woe, to those who take arms in favor of the Mamelukes and fight against us! There will be no hope for them; they will perish!

Sheiks, Ulemans, believers of Mohammed, make known to the people that those who have been enemies to me will find no refuge either in this world or the other. Is there a man so blind as not to see that Destiny itself directs my operations?"

In 1814 France faced overwhelming odds and Napoleon was forced to abdicate. Before his exile to Elba he bade farewell to the Old Guard on 20th April 1814 at Fontainebleau:

"Soldiers of my Old Guard: I bid you farewell. For twenty years I have constantly accompanied you on the road to honour and glory. In these latter times, as in the days of our prosperity, you have invariably been models of courage and fidelity. With men such as you our cause could not be lost; but the war would have been interminable; it would have been civil war, and that would have entailed deeper misfortunes on France.

I have sacrificed all of my interests to those of the country.

I go, but you, my friends, will continue to serve France. Her happiness was my only thought. It will still be the object of my wishes. Do not regret my fate; if I have consented to survive, it is to serve your glory. I intend to write the history of the great achievements we have performed together. Adieu, my friends. Would I could press you all to my heart."

In February 1815 Napoleon escaped from Elba and on returning to the French mainland addressed his loyal troops:

"Soldiers, behold the officers of battalion who have accompanied me in my misfortune: they are all my friends; they are dear to my heart. Every time I saw them, they represented to me the several regiments of the army. Among these six hundred brave men, there are soldiers of every regiment; all brought me back those great days whose memory is so dear to me, for all were covered with honourable scars received in those memorable battles. In loving them, it is you all, soldiers of the French army, that I loved."

They bring you back these eagles; let them be your rallying-point. In giving them to the Guard, I give them to the whole army. Treachery and untoward circumstances had wrapped them in a shroud; but, thanks to the French people and to you, they reappear resplendent in all their glory. Swear that they shall always be found when and wherever the interest of the country may call them! Let the traitors and those who would invade our territory, be never able to endure their gaze."

Admiral Lord Horatio Nelson

At 11.45 am as the British fleet closed with the opposing combined fleets of France and Spain on 21 October for the Battle of Trafalgar, Admiral Lord Nelson signalled all the necessary battle instructions to his ships. However, aware of the momentousness of events to come, Lord Nelson felt that something extra was required. He instructed his signal officer, Lieutenant John Pasco, to signal to the fleet, as quickly as possible, the message. Pasco takes up the story in his own words:

'His Lordship came to me on the poop, and after ordering certain signals to be made, about a quarter to noon, he said, 'Mr. Pasco, I wish to say to the fleet, ENGLAND CONFIDES THAT EVERY MAN WILL DO HIS DUTY' and he added 'You must be quick, for I have one more to make which is for close action.' I replied, 'If your Lordship will permit me to substitute the confides for expects the signal will soon be completed, because the word expects is in the vocabulary, and confides must be spelt,' His Lordship replied, in haste, and with seeming satisfaction, 'That will do, Pasco, make it directly.'

"England expects every man to do his duty"

Duke of Wellington

The Battle of Waterloo (18 June 1815) produced a number of memorable quotes from the great general.

"Napoleon has humbugged me, by God;
he has gained twenty-four hours march on me."

"Up Guards and at them again."

At a key point in the battle when victory could have gone to either side, Wellington was in dire need of the arrival of Blücher and his Prussian troops to swing balance in his favour.

"Give me night or give me Blücher."

"It has been a damned serious business...Blücher and I have lost 30,000 men. It has been a damned nice thing – the nearest thing you saw in your life...By God! I don't think it would have been done if I had not been there."

Giuseppe Garibaldi

Garibaldi (1807-1882) was an Italian patriot, master of guerrilla warfare and military leader who helped free the Italians from the rule of Austria and unify the country. In 1860, Garibaldi's thousand "red shirts" took Sicily in the name of Victor Emmanuel II of Italy and then crossed to the mainland. The speech below is the eloquent appeal he made to his soldiers in 1860:

"My comrades in arms

We must now consider the period which is just drawing to a close as almost the last stage of our national resurrection, and prepare ourselves to finish worthily the marvellous design of the elect of twenty generations, the completion of which Providence has reserved for this fortunate age.

Yes, young men, Italy owes to you an undertaking which has merited the applause of the universe. You have conquered and you will conquer still, because you are prepared for the tactics that decide the fate of battles. You are not unworthy of the men who entered the ranks of a Macedonian phalanx, and who contended not in vain with the proud conquerors of Asia. To this wonderful page in our country's history another more glorious still will be added, and the slave shall show at last to his free brothers a sharpened sword forged from the links of his fetters.

To arms, then, all of you! All of you! And the oppressors and the mighty shall disappear like dust. You, too, women, cast away all the cowards from your embraces; they will give you only cowards for children, and you who are the daughters of the land of beauty must bear children who are noble and brave. Let timid doctrinaires depart from among us to carry their servility and their miserable fears elsewhere. This people is its own master. It wishes to be the brother of other peoples, but to look on the insolent with a proud glance, not to grovel before them imploring its own freedom. It will no longer follow in the trail of men whose hearts are foul. No! No! No!

Providence has presented Italy with Victor Emmanuel. Every Italian should rally round him. By the side of Victor Emmanuel every quarrel should be forgotten, all rancour depart. Once more I repeat my battle-cry: "To arms, all – all of you!" If March, 1861, does not find one million Italians in arms, then alas for liberty, alas for the life of Italy. Ah, no, far be from me a thought which I loathe like poison. March of 1861, or if need be February, will find us all at our post – Italians of Calatafimi, Palermo, Ancona, the Volturno, Castelfidardo, and Isernia – and with us every man of this land who is not a coward or a slave. Let all of us rally round the glorious hero of Palestro and give the last blow to the crumbling edifice of tyranny. Receive, then, my gallant young volunteers, at the honoured conclusion of ten battles, one word of farewell from me.

I utter this word with deepest affection and from the very bottom of my heart. Today I am obliged to retire, but for a few days only. The hour of battle will find me with you again, by the side of the champions of Italian liberty. Let those only return to their homes who are called by the imperative duties which they owe to their families, and those who by their glorious wounds have deserved the credit of their country. These, indeed, will serve Italy in their homes by their counsel, by the very aspect of the scars which adorn their youthful brows. Apart from these, let all others remain to guard our glorious banners. We shall meet again before long to march together to the redemption of our brothers who are still slaves of the stranger. We shall meet again before long to march to new triumphs."

General Montgomery

In World War II, after a series of defeats in N Africa by the Germans under Field Marshal Rommel, the British Army had been driven so far eastwards that they were within sixty miles of the Nile. Under these difficult circumstances General Montgomery was given command of the Allied 8th Army in North Africa in August 1942 and addressed his officers as follows:

"I want first of all to introduce myself to you. You do not know me. . . . I have only been here a few hours. But from what I have seen and heard since I arrived I am prepared to say . . . I have confidence in you. . . . I believe that one of the first duties of a commander is to create what I call "atmosphere," and in that atmosphere his staff, subordinate commanders, and troops will live and work and fight. I do not like the general atmosphere I find here. It is an atmosphere of doubt, of looking back to select the next place to which to withdraw, of loss of confidence in our ability to defeat Rommel, of desperate defence measures by reserves in preparing positions in Cairo and the Delta. All that must cease. . . . Now I understand that Rommel is expected to attack at any moment. Excellent. Let him attack. . . Meanwhile, we ourselves will start to plan a great offensive; it will be the beginning of a campaign which will hit Rommel and his army for six right out of Africa. . . . The great point to remember is that we are going to finish with this chap Rommel once and for all. It will be quite easy. There is no doubt about it. He is definitely a nuisance. Therefore we will hit him a crack and finish with him."

Douglas Bader

In 1939, eight years after a flying accident resulted in the loss of both his legs and consequent retirement from the RAF, Flight Commander Douglas Bader persuaded the authorities that he was capable of active service. Remarkably, he went on to be a World War II fighter ace, and trained his squadron with three basic rules for aerial combat:

"If you have the height, you control the battle.
If you come out of the sun, the enemy cannot see you.
If you hold your fire until you are very close, you seldom miss."

General Dwight D. Eisenhower

Supreme Commander of the Allied Forces in Europe, in charge of planning and executing the invasion of France for the ultimate liberation of Europe from Hitler's power. Speech to troops before D-Day in June 1944:

"Soldiers, Sailors and Airmen of the Allied Expeditionary Forces:
You are about to embark upon the Great Crusade, toward which we have striven these many months. The eyes of the world are upon you. The hopes and prayers of liberty-loving people everywhere march with you.

In company with our brave Allies and brothers-in-arms on other Fronts, you will bring about the destruction of the German war machine, the elimination of Nazi tyranny over the oppressed peoples of Europe, and security for ourselves in a free world.

Your task will not be an easy one. Your enemy is well trained, well equipped and battle hardened. He will fight savagely. But this is the year 1944! Much has happened since the Nazi triumphs of 1940-41. The United Nations have inflicted upon the Germans great defeats, in open battle, man-to-man. Our air offensive has seriously reduced their strength in the air and their capacity to wage war on the ground. Our Home Fronts have given us an overwhelming superiority in weapons and munitions of war, and placed at our disposal great reserves of trained fighting men.

The tide has turned! The free men of the world are marching together to Victory!

I have full confidence in your courage and devotion to duty and skill in battle. We will accept nothing less than full Victory!

Good luck! And let us beseech the blessing of Almighty God upon this great and noble undertaking."

US General George Patton

Old "Blood and Guts" was one of the most colourful and charismatic generals of World War II as this speech demonstrates. It was given in England on June 5th, 1944 prior to Patton taking his troops to France after the Allied invasion of Normandy. This is such a remarkable speech that it is quoted in its entirety:

"Men, this stuff that some sources sling around about America wanting out of this war, not wanting to fight, is a crock of bullshit. Americans love to fight, traditionally. All real Americans love the sting and clash of battle. You are here today for three reasons. First, because you are here to defend your homes and your loved ones. Second, you are here for your own self respect, because you would not want to be anywhere else. Third, you are here because you are real men and all real men like to fight. When you, here, everyone of you, were kids, you all admired the champion marble player, the fastest runner, the toughest boxer, the big league ball players, and the All-American football players. Americans love a winner. Americans will not tolerate a loser. Americans despise cowards. Americans play to win all of the time. I wouldn't give a hoot in hell for a man who lost and laughed. That's why Americans have never lost nor will ever lose a war; for the very idea of losing is hateful to an American.

You are not all going to die. Only two percent of you right here today would die in a major battle. Death must not be feared. Death, in time, comes to all men. Yes, every man is scared in his first battle. If he says he's not, he's a liar. Some men are cowards but they fight the same as the brave men or they get the hell slammed out of them watching men fight who are just as scared as they are. The real hero is the man who fights even though he is scared. Some men get over their fright in a minute under fire. For some, it takes an hour. For some, it takes days. But a real man will never let his fear of death overpower his honor, his sense of duty to his country, and his innate manhood. Battle is the most magnificent competition in which a human being can indulge. It brings out all that is best and it removes all that is base. Americans pride themselves on being He Men and they ARE He Men. Remember that the enemy is just as frightened as you are, and probably more so. They are not supermen.

All through your Army careers, you men have bitched about what you call "chicken shit drilling". That, like everything else in this Army, has a definite purpose. That purpose is alertness. Alertness must be bred into every soldier. I don't give a fuck for a man who's not always on his toes. You men are veterans or you wouldn't be here. You are ready for what's to come. A man must be alert at all times if he expects to stay alive. If you're not alert, sometime, a German son-of-an-asshole-bitch is going to sneak up behind you and beat you to death with a sockful of shit!

There are four hundred neatly marked graves somewhere in Sicily all because one man went to sleep on the job. But they are German graves, because we caught the bastard asleep before they did. An Army is a team. It lives, sleeps, eats, and fights as a team. This individual heroic stuff is pure horse shit. The bilious bastards who write that kind of stuff for the Saturday Evening Post don't know any more about real fighting under fire than they know about fucking!

We have the finest food, the finest equipment, the best spirit, and the best men in the world. Why, by God, I actually pity those poor sons-of-bitches we're going up against. By God, I do.

My men don't surrender. I don't want to hear of any soldier under my command being captured unless he has been hit. Even if you are hit, you can still fight back. That's not just bullshit either. The kind of man that I want in my command is just like the lieutenant in Libya, who, with a Luger against his chest, jerked off his helmet, swept the gun aside with one hand, and busted the hell out of the Kraut with his helmet. Then he jumped on the gun and went out and killed another German before they knew what the hell was coming off. And, all of that time, this man had a bullet through a lung. There was a real man!

All of the real heroes are not storybook combat fighters, either. Every single man in this Army plays a vital role. Don't ever let up. Don't ever think that your job is unimportant. Every man has a job to do and he must do it. Every man is a vital link in the great chain. What if every truck driver suddenly decided that he didn't like the whine of those shells overhead, turned yellow, and jumped headlong into a ditch? The cowardly bastard could say, "Hell, they won't miss me, just one man in thousands". But, what if every man thought that way? Where in the hell would we be now? What would our country, our loved ones, our homes, even the world, be like? No, Goddamnit, Americans don't think like that. Every man does his job. Every man serves the whole. Every department, every unit, is important in the vast scheme of this war. The ordnance men are needed to supply the guns and machinery of war to keep us rolling. The Quartermaster is needed to bring up food and clothes because where we are going there isn't a hell of a lot to steal. Every last man on K.P. has a job to do, even the one who heats our water to keep us from getting the 'G.I. Shits'.

Each man must not think only of himself, but also of his buddy fighting beside him. We don't want yellow cowards in this Army. They should be killed off like rats. If not, they will go home after this war and breed more cowards. The brave men will breed more brave men. Kill off the Goddamned cowards and we will have a nation of brave men.

One of the bravest men that I ever saw was a fellow on top of a telegraph pole in the midst of a furious fire fight in Tunisia. I stopped and asked what the hell he was doing up there at a time like that. He answered, "Fixing the wire, Sir". I asked, "Isn't that a little unhealthy right about now?" He answered, "Yes Sir, but the Goddamned wire has to be fixed". I asked, "Don't those planes strafing the road bother you?" And he answered, "No, Sir, but you sure as hell do!" Now, there was a real man. A real soldier. There was a man who devoted all he had to his duty, no matter how seemingly insignificant his duty might appear at the time, no matter how great the odds. And you should have seen those trucks on the road to Tunisia. Those drivers were magnificent. All day and all night they rolled over those son-of-a-bitching roads, never stopping, never faltering from their course, with shells bursting all around them all of the time. We got through on good old American guts. Many of those men drove for over forty consecutive hours. These men weren't combat men, but they were soldiers with a job to do. They did it, and in one hell of a way they did it. They were part of a team. Without team effort, without them, the fight would have been lost. All of the links in the chain pulled together and the chain became unbreakable.

Don't forget, you men don't know that I'm here. No mention of that fact is to be made in any letters. The world is not supposed to know what the hell happened to me. I'm not supposed to be commanding this Army. I'm not even supposed to be here in England. Let the first bastards to find out be the Goddamned Germans. Some day I want to see them rise up on their piss-soaked hind legs and howl, 'Jesus Christ, it's the Goddamned Third Army again and that son-of-a-fucking-bitch Patton'.

We want to get the hell over there. The quicker we clean up this Goddamned mess, the quicker we can take a little jaunt against the purple pissing Japs and clean out their nest, too. Before the Goddamned Marines get all of the credit."

Sure, we want to go home. We want this war over with. The quickest way to get it over with is to go get the bastards who started it. The quicker they are whipped, the quicker we can go home. The shortest way home is through Berlin and Tokyo. And when we get to Berlin, I am personally going to shoot that paper hanging son-of-a-bitch Hitler. Just like I'd shoot a snake!

When a man is lying in a shell hole, if he just stays there all day, a German will get to him eventually. The hell with that idea. The hell with taking it. My men don't dig foxholes. I don't want them to. Foxholes only slow up an offensive. Keep moving. And don't give the enemy time to dig one either. We'll win this war, but we'll win it only by fighting and by showing the Germans that we've got more guts than they have; or ever will have. We're not going to just shoot the sons-of-bitches, we're going to rip out their living Goddamned guts and use them to grease the treads of our tanks. We're going to murder those lousy Hun cocksuckers by the bushel-fucking-basket. War is a bloody, killing business. You've got to spill their blood, or they will spill yours. Rip them up the belly. Shoot them in the guts. When shells are hitting all around you and you wipe the dirt off your face and realize that instead of dirt it's the blood and guts of what once was your best friend beside you, you'll know what to do!

I don't want to get any messages saying, "I am holding my position." We are not holding a Goddamned thing. Let the Germans do that. We are advancing constantly and we are not interested in holding onto anything, except the enemy's balls. We are going to twist his balls and kick the living shit out of him all of the time. Our basic plan of operation is to advance and to keep on advancing regardless of whether we have to go over, under, or through the enemy. We are going to go through him like crap through a goose; like shit through a tin horn!

From time to time there will be some complaints that we are pushing our people too hard. I don't give a good Goddamn about such complaints. I believe in the old and sound rule that an ounce of sweat will save a gallon of blood. The harder WE push, the more Germans we will kill. The more Germans we kill, the fewer of our men will be killed. Pushing means fewer casualties. I want you all to remember that.

There is one great thing that you men will all be able to say after this war is over and you are home once again. You may be thankful that twenty years from now when you are sitting by the fireplace with your grandson on your knee and he asks you what you did in the great World War II, you WON'T have to cough, shift him to the other knee and say, "Well, your Granddaddy shoveled shit in Louisiana." No, Sir, you can look him straight in the eye and say, "Son, your Granddaddy rode with the Great Third Army and a Son-of-a-Goddamned-Bitch named Georgie Patton!"

Colonel Tim Collins OBE

As Commanding Officer of the 1st Battalion Royal Irish Regiment prior to invasion of Iraq in 2003 Tim Collins' inspiring eve of battle speech to his regiment rightly caught the public's imagination:

"We go to liberate, not to conquer. We will not fly our flags in their country.

We are entering Iraq to free a people and the only flag which will be flown in that ancient land is their own. Show respect for them.

There are some who are alive at this moment who will not be alive shortly.

Those who do not wish to go on that journey, we will not send.

As for the others, I expect you to rock their world. Wipe them out if that is what they choose. But if you are ferocious in battle remember to be magnanimous in victory.

Iraq is steeped in history. It is the site of the Garden of Eden, of the Great Flood and the birthplace of Abraham.

Tread lightly there.

You will see things that no man could pay to see – and you will have to go a long way to find a more decent, generous and upright people than the Iraqis.

You will be embarrassed by their hospitality even though they have nothing.

Don't treat them as refugees for they are in their own country. Their children will be poor, in years to come they will know that the light of liberation in their lives was brought by you.

If there are casualties of war then remember that when they woke up and got dressed in the morning they did not plan to die this day. Allow them dignity in death. Bury them properly and mark their graves.

It is my foremost intention to bring every single one of you out alive. But there may be people among us who will not see the end of this campaign. We will put them in their sleeping bags

and send them back. There will be no time for sorrow.
The enemy should be in no doubt that we are his nemesis and
that we are bringing about his rightful destruction.
There are many regional commanders who have stains on their
souls and they are stoking the fires of hell for Saddam. He and
his forces will be destroyed by this coalition for what they
have done.
As they die they will know their deeds have brought them to
this place. Show them no pity.
It is a big step to take another human life. It is not to be done
lightly.
I know of men who have taken life needlessly in other
conflicts. I can assure you they live with the mark of Cain
upon them.
If someone surrenders to you then remember they have that
right in international law and ensure that one day they go
home to their family.
The ones who wish to fight, well, we aim to please.
If you harm the regiment or its history by over-enthusiasm in
killing or in cowardice, know it is your family who will suffer.
You will be shunned unless your conduct is of the highest – for
your deeds will follow you down through history. We will
bring shame on neither our uniform nor our nation.
(Referring to Saddam Hussein's chemical and biological
weapons.)
It is not a question of if, it's a question of when. We know he
has already devolved the decision to lower commanders, and
that means he has already taken the decision himself.
If we survive the first strike we will survive the attack.
As for ourselves, let's bring everyone home and leave Iraq a
better place for us having been there.
Our business now is north."

Howard Leedham

British former Special Forces officer Howard Leedham's tactical guidance for the Pakistani Pathan militia tribesmen he was commissioned by the US State Department to train for covert anti-terrorist activities in 2004:

"On your way to the target, stealth is everything; speed is nothing. When you hit a target, speed is everything, stealth is nothing. Know compassion for those who are harmless, know severity to those who are harmful. He who hesitates is dead. Always be better than your enemy, he only has to be better than you once. Look after each other. God speed and may the blessings of Allah be upon you. It has been my honour to serve with you."

THE HOME FRONT POLITICAL LEADERSHIP

"It's not good enough that we do our best; sometimes we have to do what's required."

Winston Churchill

Julius Ceasar

After his conquests of Gaul, the Rhine and Britain, Julius Ceasar was ordered by the Senate in Rome to disband his army and surrender his status as governor. He refused and was ordered back to Rome to stand trial. In 49BC he brought his army to the Northern Italian boundary of Rome – marked by the River Rubicon, which he then crossed, commenting:

"Alea iacta est."
(*The die is cast*).

His invasion of his homeland sparked a civil war from which he emerged victorious.

Alexander the Great

Alexander, King of Macedonia, was one of the greatest ever military geniuses. He invaded Asia Minor in 334BC, conquering all who stood in his way including the dominant Persians. He covered such vast distances – as far east as Punjab – that he had to exhort his reluctant troops to follow him into what were then strange and far distant lands:

"I observe, gentlemen, that when I would lead you on a new venture you no longer follow me with your old spirit. I have asked you to meet me that we may come to a decision together: are we, upon my advice, to go forward, or, upon yours, to turn back?

If you have any complaint to make about the results of your efforts hitherto, or about myself as your commander, there is no more to say... With all that accomplished, why do you hesitate to extend the power of Macedon – your power – to the Hyphasis and the tribes on the other side? Are you afraid that a few natives who may still be left will offer opposition? Come, come! These natives either surrender without a blow or are caught on the run – or leave their country undefended for your taking; and when we take it, we make a present of it to those who have joined us of their own free will and fight on our side.

For a man who is a man, work, in my belief, if it is directed to noble ends, has no object beyond itself; none the less, if any of you wish to know what limit may be set to this particular campaign, let me tell you that the area of country still ahead of us, from here to the Ganges and the Eastern ocean, is comparatively small...

But if you turn back now, there will remain unconquered many warlike peoples between the Hyphasis and the Eastern Ocean, and many more to the northward and the Hyrcanian Sea, with the Scythians, too, not far away; so that if we withdraw now there is a danger that the territory which we do not yet securely hold may be stirred to revolt by some nation or other we have not yet forced into submission. Should that happen, all that we have done and suffered will have proved fruitless–or we shall be faced with the task of doing it over again from the beginning. Gentlemen of Macedon, and you, my friends and allies, this must not be.

Stand firm; for well you know that hardship and danger are the price of glory, and that sweet is the savour of a life of courage and of deathless renown beyond the grave...

I could not have blamed you for being the first to lose heart if I, your commander, had not shared in your exhausting marches and your perilous campaigns; it would have been natural enough if you had done all the work merely for others to reap the reward. But it is not so. You and I, gentlemen, have shared the labour and shared the danger, and the rewards are for us all. The conquered territory belongs to you; from your ranks the governors of it are chosen; already the greater part of its treasure passes into your hands, and when all Asia is overrun, then indeed I will go further than the mere satisfaction of our ambitions: the utmost hopes of riches or power which each one of you cherishes will be far surpassed, and whoever wishes to return home will be allowed to go, either with me or without me. I will make those who stay the envy of those who return."

Patrick Henry

American orator and politician, who led independence for Virginia in the 1770s. This speech was made on 23 March 1775 at the House of Burgesses, Richmond, Virginia, to encourage mobilisation against the British. Not recorded at the time, it was reconstructed some years after and is immortal for its final words:

"They tell us, sir, that we are weak; unable to cope with so formidable an adversary. But when shall we be stronger? Will it be the next week, or the next year? Will it be when we are totally disarmed, and when a British guard shall be stationed in every house? Shall we gather strength by irresolution and inaction? Shall we acquire the means of effectual resistance by lying supinely on our backs and hugging the delusive phantom of hope, until our enemies shall have bound us hand and foot? Sir, we are not weak if we make a proper use of those means which the God of nature hath placed in our power. The millions of people, armed in the holy cause of liberty, and in such a country as that which we possess, are invincible by any force which our enemy can send against us. Besides, sir, we shall not fight our battles alone. There is a just God who presides over the destinies of nations, and who will raise up friends to fight our battles for us. The battle, sir, is not to the strong alone; it is to the vigilant, the active, the brave. Besides, sir, we have no election. If we were base enough to desire it, it is now too late to retire from the contest. There is no retreat but in submission and slavery! Our chains are forged! Their clanking may be heard on the plains of Boston! The war is inevitable—and let it come! I repeat it, sir, let it come.

It is in vain, sir, to extenuate the matter. Gentlemen may cry, Peace, Peace— but there is no peace. The war is actually begun! The next gale that sweeps from the north will bring to our ears the clash of resounding arms! Our brethren are already in the field! Why stand we here idle? What is it that gentlemen wish? What would they have? Is life so dear, or peace so sweet, as to be purchased at the price of chains and slavery? Forbid it, Almighty God!"

I know not what course others may take; but as for me, give me liberty or give me death."

Postscript to this speech: On 27th September 1942 US President Roosevelt launched the SS *Patrick Henry* and thirteen other ships quoting the last "Give me liberty or give me death" lines from Henry's speech. This why these speedily produced ships, (2,710 of them) that were so essential to the World War II, were known as 'Liberty Ships'.

Otto von Bismarck

In 1862 the German Chancellor Otto von Bismarck had to convince the reluctant Prussian Landtag that increased military spending and preparedness was in the interests of a unified Germany. This is his 'Blood and Iron' speech:

"The Conflict is viewed too tragically, and presented too tragically in the press; the regime does not seek war. If the crisis can be ended with honour, the regime will gladly do so. The great independence of the individual makes it difficult in Prussia to rule under the Constitution. In France it is otherwise; there, individual independence is lacking. The constitutional crisis, however, is no shame, but rather an honour. We are perhaps too educated to put up with a constitution - we are too critical. Public opinion wavers; the press is not public opinion; we know how that arises. There are too many Catilines*, who have revolution at heart.

The members [of the House], however, have the task of standing over public sentiment, and of guiding it. Our blood is too hot, we prefer armour too great for our small body to carry, but we should put it to service. Germany does not look to Prussia's liberalism, but to its power. Bavaria, Wurttemberg, and Baden would like to turn to liberalism, but they shall not assume Prussia's role. Prussia must collect its forces for the favourable occasion, which has several times been neglected; Prussia's borders are not favourable to a healthy national life. Not by speeches and decisions of majorities will the greatest problems of the time be decided - that was the mistake of 1848-49 - but by iron and blood. This olive branch (he drew it from his memorandum book) I picked up in Avignon, to offer, as a symbol of peace, to the popular party: I see, however, that it is still not the time for it."

* From Lucius Sergius Catilina (108BC-62BC) – conspirator who attempted to overthrow the power of the Roman Senate.

William Tecumseh Sherman

Union general – American Civil War (1861–1865):

"If nominated, I will not run; if elected, I will not serve."

"If forced to choose between the penitentiary and the White House for four years, I would say the penitentiary, thank you."

President Abraham Lincoln

Lincoln's Gettysburg address was made on 19 November 1863 during the American Civil War at the dedication of the Soldiers' National Cemetery. Although it is perhaps one of the most famous of all American speeches, there are at least five known written versions and this is the only one to which Lincoln affixed his signature, and the last he is known to have written:

"Four score and seven years ago our fathers brought forth on this continent a new nation, conceived in liberty, and dedicated to the proposition that all men are created equal.

Now we are engaged in a great civil war, testing whether that nation, or any nation, so conceived and so dedicated, can long endure. We are met on a great battle-field of that war. We have come to dedicate a portion of that field, as a final resting place for those who here gave their lives that that nation might live. It is altogether fitting and proper that we should do this.

But, in a larger sense, we can not dedicate, we can not consecrate, we can not hallow this ground. The brave men, living and dead, who struggled here, have consecrated it, far above our poor power to add or detract. The world will little note, nor long remember what we say here, but it can never forget what they did here. It is for us the living, rather, to be dedicated here to the unfinished work which they who fought here have thus far so nobly advanced. It is rather for us to be here dedicated to the great task remaining before us—that from these honored dead we take increased devotion to that cause for which they gave the last full measure of devotion— that we here highly resolve that these dead shall not have died in vain—that this nation, under God, shall have a new birth of freedom—and that government of the people, by the people, for the people, shall not perish from the earth."

David Lloyd George

British Prime Minister on the causes of the Great War – June 1917:

"It is a satisfaction for Britain in these terrible times that no share of the responsibility for these events rests on her.

She is not the Jonah in this storm. The part taken by our country in this conflict, in its origin, and in its conduct, has been as honourable and chivalrous as any part ever taken in any country in any operation.

We might imagine from declarations which were made by the Germans, aye! and even by a few people in this country, who are constantly referring to our German comrades, that this terrible war was wantonly and wickedly provoked by England – never Scotland – never Wales – and never Ireland. Wantonly provoked by England to increase her possessions, and to destroy the influence, the power, and the prosperity of a dangerous rival.

There never was a more foolish travesty of the actual facts. It happened three years ago, or less, but there have been so many bewildering events crowded into those intervening years that some people might have forgotten, perhaps, some of the essential facts, and it is essential that we should now and again restate them, not merely to refute the calumniators of our native land, but in order to sustain the hearts of her people by the unswerving conviction that no part of the guilt of this terrible bloodshed rests on the conscience of their native land.

What are the main facts? There were six countries which entered the war at the beginning. Britain was last, and not the first.

Before she entered the war Britain made every effort to avoid it; begged, supplicated, and entreated that there should be no conflict.

I was a member of the Cabinet at the time, and I remember the earnest endeavours we made to persuade Germany and Austria not to precipitate Europe into this welter of blood. We begged them to summon a European conference to consider.

Had that conference met, arguments against provoking such a catastrophe were so overwhelming that there would never have been a war. Germany knew that, so she rejected the conference, although Austria was prepared to accept it. She suddenly declared war, and yet we are the people who wantonly provoked this war, in order to attack Germany.

We begged Germany not to attack Belgium, and produced a treaty, signed by the King of Prussia, as well as the King of England, pledging himself to protect Belgium against an invader, and we said, "If you invade Belgium we shall have no alternative but to defend it."

The enemy invaded Belgium, and now they say, "Why, forsooth, you, England, provoked this war."
It is not quite the story of the wolf and the lamb. I will tell you why - because Germany expected to find a lamb and found a lion."

Adolf Hitler

Landsberg, 5 November 1925:

"If freedom is short of weapons, we must compensate with willpower."

General Charles de Gaulle

The Word War II Commander of the Free French Forces broadcast from Britain on the BBC to France, 18 June 1940, exhorting the French people to resist the German Nazi regime as the French government prepared to sign an armistice with the Nazi invaders:

"The French government, after having asked for an armistice, now knows the conditions dictated by the enemy.

The result of these conditions would be the complete demobilisation of the French land, sea, and air forces, the surrender of our weapons and the total occupation of French territory. The French government would come under German and Italian tutelage.

It may therefore be said that this armistice would not only be a capitulation, but that it would also reduce the country to slavery. Now, a great many Frenchmen refuse to accept either capitulation or slavery, for reasons which are called: honour, common sense, and the higher interests of the country.

I say honour, for France has undertaken not to lay down arms save in agreement with her allies. As long as the allies continue the war, her government has no right to surrender to the enemy. The Polish, Norwegian, Belgian, Netherlands, and

Luxemburg governments, though driven from their territories, have thus interpreted their duty.

I say common sense, for it is absurd to consider the struggle as lost. True, we have suffered a major defeat. We lost the battle of France through a faulty military system, mistakes in the conduct of operations, and the defeatist spirit shown by the government during recent battles. But we still have a vast empire, our fleet is intact, and we possess large sums in gold. We still have allies, who possess immense resources and who dominate the seas. We still have the gigantic potentialities of American industry. The same war conditions which caused us to be beaten by 5,000 planes and 6,000 tanks can tomorrow bring victory by means of 20,000 tanks and 20,000 planes.

I say the higher interests of the country, for this is not a Franco-German war to be decided by a single battle. This is a world war. No one can foresee whether the neutral countries of today will not be at war tomorrow, or whether Germany's allies will always remain her allies. If the powers of freedom ultimately triumph over those of servitude, what will be the fate of a France which has submitted to the enemy?

Honour, common sense, and the interests of the country require that all free Frenchmen, wherever they be, should continue the fight as best they may.

It is therefore necessary to group the largest possible French force wherever this can be done. Everything which can be collected by way of French military elements and potentialities for armaments production must be organised wherever such elements exist.

I, General de Gaulle, am undertaking this national task here in England.

I call upon all French servicemen of the land, sea, and air

forces; I call upon French engineers and skilled armaments workers who are on British soil, or have the means of getting here, to come and join me.

I call upon the leaders, together with all soldiers, sailors, and airmen of the French land, sea, and air forces, wherever they may now be, to get in touch with me.

I call upon all Frenchmen who want to remain free to listen to my voice and follow me.

Long live free France in honour and independence!"

Vyacheslav Molotov

A leading figure of the Russian Soviet government, Molotov was signatory to the 1939 non-aggression treaty between Germany and Russia (Molotov-Ribbentrop Pact). When it was broken by Germany's invasion of the Soviet Union on 22 June 1941 he, rather than the Russian leader Stalin, announced the news:

Citizens of the Soviet Union.

The Soviet Government and its head, Comrade Stalin, have authorized me to make the following statement:

Today at 4 o'clock a.m., without any claims having been presented to the Soviet Union, without a declaration of war, German troops attacked our country, attacked our borders at many points and bombed from their airplanes our cities; Zhitomir, Kiev, Sevastopol, Kaunas and some others, killing and wounding over two hundred persons.

There were also enemy air raids and artillery shelling from Rumanian and Finnish territory.

This unheard of attack upon our country is perfidy unparalleled in the history of civilized nations. The attack on our country was perpetrated despite the fact that a treaty of non-aggression had been signed between the U. S. S. R. and Germany and that the Soviet Government most faithfully abided by all provisions of this treaty.

The attack upon our country was perpetrated despite the fact that during the entire period of operation of this treaty, the German Government could not find grounds for a single complaint against the U.S.S.R. as regards observance of this treaty.

Entire responsibility for this predatory attack upon the Soviet Union falls fully and completely upon the German Fascist rulers.

At 5:30 a.m. — that is, after the attack had already been perpetrated, Von der Schulenburg, the German Ambassador in Moscow, on behalf of his government made the statement to me as People's Commissar of Foreign Affairs to the effect that the German Government had decided to launch war against the U.S.S.R. in connection with the concentration of Red Army units near the eastern German frontier.

In reply to this I stated on behalf of the Soviet Government that, until the very last moment, the German Government had not presented any claims to the Soviet Government, that Germany attacked the U.S.S.R. despite the peaceable position of the Soviet Union, and that for this reason Fascist Germany is the aggressor.

On instruction of the government of the Soviet Union I also stated that at no point had our troops or our air force committed a violation of the frontier and therefore the statement made this morning by the Rumanian radio to the effect that Soviet aircraft allegedly had fired on Rumanian airdromes is a sheer lie and provocation.

Likewise a lie and provocation is the whole declaration made today by Hitler, who is trying belatedly to concoct accusations charging the Soviet Union with failure to observe the Soviet-German pact.

Now that the attack on the Soviet Union has already been committed, the Soviet Government has ordered our troops to repulse the predatory assault and to drive German troops from the territory of our country.

This war has been forced upon us, not by the German people, not by German workers, peasants and intellectuals, whose sufferings we well understand, but by the clique of bloodthirsty Fascist rulers of Germany who have enslaved Frenchmen, Czechs, Poles, Serbians, Norway, Belgium, Denmark, Holland, Greece and other nations.

The government of the Soviet Union expresses its unshakable confidence that our valiant army and navy and brave falcons of the Soviet Air Force will acquit themselves with honor in performing their duty to the fatherland and to the Soviet people, and will inflict a crushing blow upon the aggressor. This is not the first time that our people have had to deal with an attack of an arrogant foe. At the time of Napoleon's invasion of Russia our people's reply was war for the fatherland, and Napoleon suffered defeat and met his doom.

It will be the same with Hitler, who in his arrogance has proclaimed a new crusade against our country. The Red Army and our whole people will again wage victorious war for the fatherland, for our country, for honor, for liberty.

The government of the Soviet Union expresses the firm conviction that the whole population of our country, all workers, peasants and intellectuals, men and women, will conscientiously perform their duties and do their work. Our entire people must now stand solid and united as never before. Each one of us must demand of himself and of others discipline, organization and self-denial worthy of real Soviet patriots, in order to provide for all the needs of the Red Army, Navy and Air Force, to insure victory over the enemy.

The government calls upon you, citizens of the Soviet Union, to rally still more closely around our glorious Bolshevist party, around our Soviet Government, around our great leader and comrade, Stalin. Ours is a righteous cause. The enemy shall be defeated. Victory will be ours."

Adolf Hitler

Hitler addressed the German Reichstag on 11 December 1941 – justifying his declaration war on the USA that very day and also explaining his previous belligerent declarations of war on Britain and Russia. It was a very long speech – here are excerpts that provide an interesting (and megalomaniac) comparison to Winston Churchill's speeches of the same period to the British Parliament:

"Deputies! Men of the German Reichstag!

A year of world-historical events is coming to an end. A year of great decisions is approaching. In this grave period I speak to you, deputies of the Reichstag, as the representatives of the German nation. In addition, the entire German nation should also review what has happened and take note of the decisions required by the present and the future.

After the repeated rejection of my peace proposal in 1940 by the British Prime Minister [Winston Churchill] and the clique that supports and controls him, it was clear by the fall of that year that this war would have to be fought through to the end, contrary to all logic and necessity. You, my old Party comrades, know that I have always detested half-hearted or weak decisions. If Providence has deemed that the German people are not to be spared this struggle, then I am thankful that She has entrusted me with the leadership in a historic conflict that will be decisive in determining the next five hundred or one thousand years, not only of our German history, but also of the history of Europe and even of the entire world.

The German people and its soldiers work and fight today not only for themselves and their own age, but also for many generations to come. A historical task of unique dimensions has been entrusted to us by the Creator that we are now obliged to carry out...

A network of roads and rail lines has been laid out so that the connections between the Spanish frontier and Petsamo [in northern Norway] can be defended independently from the sea. The installations built by the Pioneer and construction battalions of the navy, army and air force in cooperation with the Todt Organisation are not at all inferior to those of the Westwall [along the German frontier with France]. The work to further strengthen all this continues without pause. I am determined to make this European front impregnable against any enemy attack...

During the past summer Germany was supported in this struggle above all by her Italian ally. For many months our ally Italy bore on its shoulders the main weight of a large part of British might. Only because of the enormous superiority in heavy tanks were the British able to bring about a temporary crisis in North Africa, but by March 24 of this year a small combined force of German and Italian units under the command of General Rommel began a counterattack...

While these daring actions were again securing the North African front with the blood of German and Italian soldiers, the threatening clouds of terrible danger were gathering over Europe. Compelled by bitter necessity, I decided in 1939 to at least try to create the prerequisite conditions for a general peace by eliminating the acute tension between Germany and Soviet Russia [with the German-Soviet non-aggression pact of August 23, 1939]. This was psychologically difficult because of the basic attitude toward Bolshevism of the German people and, above all, of the Party. Objectively, though, this was a simple matter because in all the countries that Britain said were threatened by us and which were offered military alliances, Germany actually had only economic interests...

I may remind you, deputies and men of the German Reichstag that, throughout the spring and summer of 1939, Britain offered military alliances to a number of countries, claiming that Germany intended to invade them and rob them of their freedom. However, the German Reich and its government could assure them with a clear conscience that these insinuations did not correspond to the truth in any way. Moreover, there was the sober military realisation that in case of a war which might be forced upon the German nation by British diplomacy, the struggle could be fought on two fronts only with very great sacrifices.

All the same, the countries involved realised very quickly – which was unfortunate for the German Reich as well – that the best and strongest guarantee against the [Soviet] threat from the East was Germany. When those countries, on their own initiative, cut their ties with the German Reich and instead put their trust in promises of aid from a power [Britain] that, in its proverbial egotism, has for centuries never given help but has always demanded it, they were thereby lost. Even so, the fate of these countries aroused the strongest sympathy of the

German people. The winter war of the Finns [against the Soviet Union, 1939-1940] aroused in us a feeling of admiration mixed with bitterness: admiration because, as a soldierly nation, we have a sympathetic heart for heroism and sacrifice, and bitterness because our concern for the enemy threat in the West and the danger in the East meant that we were no position to help. When it became clear to us that Soviet Russia concluded that the [German-Soviet] delineation [in August 1939] of political spheres of influence gave it the right to practically exterminate foreign nations, the relationship was maintained only for utilitarian reasons, contrary to reason and sentiment.

Already in 1940 it became increasingly clear from month to month that the plans of the men in the Kremlin were aimed at the domination, and thus the destruction, of all of Europe. I have already told the nation of the build-up of Soviet Russian military power in the East during a period when Germany had only a few divisions in the provinces bordering Soviet Russia. Only a blind person could fail to see that a military build-up of unique world-historical dimensions was being carried out. And this was not in order to protect something that was being threatened, but rather only to attack that which seemed incapable of defence.

The quick conclusion of the campaign in the West [1940] meant that those in power in Moscow were not able to count on the immediate exhaustion of the German Reich. However, they did not change their plans at all, but only postponed the timing of their attack. The summer of 1941 seemed like the ideal moment to strike. A new Mongol invasion was ready to pour across Europe. Mr. Churchill also promised that there would be a change in the British war against Germany at this same time. In a cowardly way, he now tries to deny, that during a secret meeting in the British House of Commons in 1940 he said that an important factor for the successful continuation and conclusion of this war would be the Soviet entry into the war, which would come during 1941 at the latest, and which would also make it possible for Britain to take the offensive. Conscious of our duty, this past spring we observed the military build-up of a world power that seemed to have inexhaustible reserves of human and material resources. Dark clouds began to gather over Europe. What is Europe, my deputies? There is no geographical definition of our continent, but only an ethnic-national and cultural one. The frontier of this continent is not the Ural Mountains, but rather the line that divides the Western outlook on life from that of the East...

Just as Rome once made her immortal contribution to the building and defence of the continent, so now have the Germanic peoples taken up the defence and protection of a family of nations which, although they may differ and diverge in their political structure and goals, nevertheless together constitute a racially and culturally unified and complementary whole.

And from this Europe there have not only been settlements in other parts of the world, but intellectual, spiritual and cultural fertilisation as well, a fact that anyone realises who is willing to acknowledge the truth rather than deny it. Thus, it was not England that cultivated the continent, but rather Anglo-Saxon and Norman branches of the Germanic nation that moved from our continent to the British island and made possible her development, which is certainly unique in history. In the same way, it was not America that discovered Europe, but the other way around. And all that which America did not get from Europe may seem worthy of admiration to a Jewified mixed race, but Europe regards that merely as symptomatic of decay in artistic and cultural life, the product of Jewish or Negroid blood mixture.

My Deputies! Men of the German Reichstag!

I have to make these remarks because this struggle, which became obviously unavoidable in the early months of this year, and which the German Reich, above all, is called upon this time to lead, also greatly transcends the interests of our own people and nation. When the Greeks once stood against the Persians, they defended more than just Greece. When the Romans stood against the Carthaginians, they defended more than just Rome. When the Roman and Germanic peoples stood together against the Huns, they defended more than just the West. When German emperors stood against the Mongols, they defended more than just Germany. And when Spanish heroes stood against Africa, they defended not just Spain, but all of Europe as well. In the same way, Germany does not fight today just for itself, but for our entire continent...

When I became aware of the possibility of a threat to the east of the Reich in 1940 through reports from the British House of Commons and by observations of Soviet Russian troop movements on our frontiers, I immediately ordered the formation of many new armoured, motorised and infantry divisions. The human and material resources for them were abundantly available. I can make only one promise to you, my deputies, and to the entire German nation: while people in democratic countries understandably talk a lot about armaments, in National Socialist Germany all the more will actually be produced. It has been that way in the past, and it is not any different now. Whenever decisive action has to be taken, we will have, with each passing year, more and, above all, better quality weapons.

We realised very clearly that under no circumstances could we allow the enemy the opportunity to strike first into our heart. Nevertheless, in this case the decision [to attack Soviet Russia] was a very difficult one. When the writers for the democratic newspapers now declare that I would have thought twice before attacking if I had known the strength of the Bolshevik adversaries, they show that they do not understand either the situation or me.

I have not sought war. To the contrary, I have done everything to avoid conflict. But I would forget my duty and my conscience if I were to do nothing in spite of the realisation that a conflict had become unavoidable. Because I regarded Soviet Russia as the gravest danger not only for the German Reich but for all of Europe, I decided, if possible, to give the order myself to attack a few days before the outbreak of this conflict...

If the German Reich, with its soldiers and weapons, had not stood against this opponent, a storm would have burned over Europe that would have eliminated, once and for all time, and in all its intellectual paucity and traditional stupidity, the laughable British idea of the European balance of power...

This is not yet the right time to speak of the planning and direction of this campaign. However, in a few sentences I would like to say something about what has been achieved [so far] in this greatest conflict in history...

As of December 1, the total number of captured Soviet Russian prisoners was 3,806,865. The number of destroyed or captured tanks was 21,391, of artillery pieces 32,541, and of airplanes 17,322. During this same period of time, 2,191 British airplanes were shot down. The navy sank 4,170,611 gross registered tons of shipping, and the air force sank 2,346,180 tons. Altogether, 6,516,791 gross registered tons were destroyed...

From June 22 to December 1 [1941], the German army has lost in this heroic struggle: 158,773 dead, 563,082 wounded and 31,191 missing. The air force has lost: 3,231 dead, 8,453 wounded and 2,028 missing. The navy: 310 dead, 232 wounded and 115 missing. For the German armed forces altogether: 162,314 dead, 571,767 wounded and 33,334 missing...

And now let me speak about another world, one that is represented by a man [President Franklin Roosevelt] who likes to chat nicely at the fireside while nations and their soldiers fight in snow and ice: above all, the man who is primarily responsible for this war...

It is a fact that the two historical conflicts between Germany and the United States were stimulated by two Americans, that is, by Presidents Woodrow Wilson and Franklin Roosevelt, although each was inspired by the same forces. History itself has rendered its verdict on Wilson. His name will always be associated with the basest betrayal in history of a pledge. The result was the ruin of national life, not only in the so-called vanquished countries, but among the victors as well. Because of this broken pledge, which alone made possible the imposed Treaty of Versailles [1919], countries were torn apart, cultures were destroyed and the economic life of all was ruined. Today we know that a group of self-serving financiers stood behind Wilson. They used this paralytic professor to lead America into a war from which they hoped to profit. The German nation once believed this man, and had to pay for this trust with political and economic ruin.

After such a bitter experience, why is there now another American president who is determined to incite wars and, above all, to stir up hostility against Germany to the point of war?...

I will overlook as meaningless the insulting attacks and rude statements by this so-called President against me personally. That he calls me a gangster is particularly meaningless, since this term did not originate in Europe, where such characters are uncommon, but in America. And aside from that, I simply cannot feel insulted by Mr. Roosevelt because I regard him, like his predecessor Woodrow Wilson, as mentally unsound.

We know that this man, with his Jewish supporters, has operated against Japan in the same way. I don't need to go into that here. The same methods were used in that case as well. This man first incites to war, and then he lies about its causes and makes baseless allegations. He repugnantly wraps himself in a cloak of Christian hypocrisy, while at the same time slowly but very steadily leading humanity into war. And finally, as an old Freemason, he calls upon God to witness that his actions are honourable. His shameless misrepresentations of truth and violations of law are unparalleled in history.

I am sure that all of you have regarded it as an act of deliverance that a country [Japan] has finally acted to protest against all this in the very way that this man had actually hoped for, and which should not surprise him now [the attack on Pearl Harbour, December 7, 1941]. After years of negotiating with this deceiver, the Japanese government finally had its fill of being treated in such a humiliating way. All of us, the German people and, I believe, all other decent people around the world as well, regard this with deep appreciation...

But whoever tries to shirk his duty has no right to be regarded as a fellow German. Just as we were pitilessly hard in the struggle for power, so also will we be just as ruthless in the struggle for the survival of our nation. During a time in which thousands of our best men, the fathers and sons of our people, have given their lives, anyone in the homeland who betrays the sacrifice on the front will forfeit his life. Regardless of the pretext with which an attempt is made to disrupt the German front, undermine the will to resist of our people, weaken the authority of the regime, or sabotage the achievements of the homeland, the guilty person will die. But with this difference: The soldier at the front who makes this sacrifice will be held in the greatest honour, whereas the person who debases this sacrifice of honour will die in disgrace.

Our opponents should not deceive themselves. In the two thousand years of recorded German history, our people have never been more determined and united than today. The Lord of the universe has been so generous to us in recent years that we bow in gratitude before a Providence that has permitted us to be members of such a great nation. We thank Him, that along with those in earlier and coming generations of the German nation, our deeds of honour may also be recorded in the eternal book of German history!

Germany's Declaration of War on America

On 11 December 1941 Germany joined her Japanese ally (four days after the Japanese attack on Pearl Harbour) and formally declared war against the United States when Reich Foreign Minister Joachim von Ribbentrop delivered a diplomatic note to the American Chargé d'Affaires in Berlin, Leland B. Morris. At the same time, the German Chargé d'Affaires in Washington, Hans Thomsen, presented a copy of this note to the Chief of the European Division of the Department of State, Ray Atherton. Here is the text of the Declaration of War:

"The government of the United States of America, having violated in the most flagrant manner and in ever increasing measure all rules of neutrality in favour of the adversaries of Germany, and having continually been guilty of the most severe provocations toward Germany ever since the outbreak of the European war, brought on by the British declaration of war against Germany on September 3, 1939, has finally resorted to open military acts of aggression.

On September 11, 1941, the President of the United States of America publicly declared that he had ordered the American Navy and Air Force to shoot on sight any German war vessel. In his speech of October 27, 1941, he once more expressly affirmed that this order was in force.

Acting under this order, American naval vessels have systematically attacked German naval forces since early September 1941. Thus, American destroyers, as for instance, the Greer, the Kearny and the Reuben James, have opened fire on German submarines according to plan. The American Secretary of the Navy, Mr. Knox, himself confirmed that the American destroyers attacked German submarines.

Furthermore, the naval forces of the United States of America, under order of their government and contrary to international law, have treated and seized German merchant ships on the high seas as enemy ships.

The German government therefore establishes the following facts:

Although Germany on her part has strictly adhered to the rules of international law in her relations with the United States of America during every period of the present war, the government of the United States of America from initial violations of neutrality has finally proceeded to open acts of war against Germany. It has thereby virtually created a state of war.

The government of the Reich consequently breaks off diplomatic relations with the United States of America and declares that under these circumstances brought about by President Roosevelt, Germany too, as from today, considers herself as being in a state of war with the United States of America."

General Douglas MacArthur

*MacArthur was commander of the US Army Forces in 1942
that had to withdraw from the Phillipines in the face of the
invading Japanese onslaught. After two years of ferocious
fighting the US landed back on the Philippines at Leyte and
MacArthur was able to make his "I Have Returned" radio
speech on 20 October, 1944:*

"This is the Voice of Freedom, General MacArthur speaking.

People of the Philippines: I have returned.

By the grace of Almighty God our forces stand again on
Philippine soil - soil consecrated in the blood of our two
peoples. We have come, dedicated and committed to the task
of destroying every vestige of enemy control over your daily
lives, and of restoring, upon a foundation of indestructible
strength, the liberties of your people.

At my side is your President, Sergio Osmena, worthy
successor of that great patriot, Manuel Quezon, with members
of his cabinet. The seat of your government is now therefore
firmly re-established on Philippine soil.

The hour of your redemption is here. Your patriots have
demonstrated an unswerving and resolute devotion to the
principles of freedom that challenges the best that is written on
the pages of human history.

I now call upon your supreme effort that the enemy may know
from the temper of an aroused and outraged people within
that he has a force there to contend with no less violent than is
the force committed from without.

Rally to me. Let the indomitable spirit of Bataan and
Corregidor lead on. As the lines of battle roll forward to bring

you within the zone of operations, rise and strike!

For future generations of your sons and daughters, strike! In the name of your sacred dead, strike!"

Fidel Castro

In the late 1950s he led the Cuban communist revolution and subsequently became dictator:

"I began the revolution with 82 men. If I had to do it again, I would do it with 10 or 15 and absolute faith. It does not matter how small you are if you have faith and a plan of action."

Che Guevara

Marxist revolutionary (1928–1967):

"The revolution is not an apple that falls when it is ripe. You have to make it fall."

Lyndon B. Johnson

American President (1963–1969):

"Once you have them by the balls, their hearts and minds will follow."

Saddam Hussein

"Call For Martyrdom"- broadcast by Iraqi Satellite Channel TV – 4 April 2003:

In the name of God, the Compassionate, the Merciful. "And fight them on until there is no more tumult." [Koranic verse]

O great people, O men of our valiant armed forces, O Iraqi young men, O mujaheedin, who carry the honour and trust of the weapons of jihad; O glorious women in your beloved, dear Baghdad, which is glorious with its people: God's peace and blessings be upon you.

The enemy, O beloved ones, is trying in vain and disappointment to confuse your steadfastness and heroic confrontation against him. Therefore, the enemy has started to cross the armed forces' defence lines around Baghdad and around other Iraqi cities.

He avoids any clash with these lines. Or he sometimes tests them. If he finds these lines steadfast and strong, with the will of God as they really are, he avoids any clash with them. Instead, he goes around them and makes a landing here or there as we had expected before. In most cases, the landing or movement is on roads in small numbers of vehicles and evil soldiers. They can be resisted and destroyed by you with the weapons you have.

You probably remember the gallant Iraqi peasant who shot down a US Apache using an old weapon. Strike at your enemy strongly. Strike at your enemy with your strong faith wherever he comes close to you.

Resist him - O people of Baghdad, the steadfast and glorious city - whenever your enemy comes close to you and dares to attack your beloved city after relying on God, the Omnipotent

Almighty. Defend your principles, nationalism, honour of men and women and faith, as well as the honour of pledge and promise.

Their dead will be in hell. Their survivors will be shrouded in disgrace. Our martyrs will be in paradise. Our survivors will be granted glory and pride.

You - O dear ones, O people of Baghdad and people of Iraq - are the banner of faith and glory. God willing, you will be victorious. God willing, they will be defeated, losers and cursed.

God is Great; pride be to God and victory be to Iraq. God is Great. Long live our nation; long live Iraq; long live Iraq; long live Palestine. Come to jihad.

Their dead will be in hell. Their survivors will be shrouded in disgrace. Our martyrs will be in paradise. Our survivors will be granted glory and pride.

May God, the merciful and compassionate, grant you - O Iraqi men and glorious women, the people of Baghdad and the people of Iraq – His glory and satisfaction.

God is great, God is great. Accursed be the criminals."

George W. Bush

After the 9/11 attacks on the US mainland in 2001 President George W Bush addressed the American nation:

"Good evening.

Today, our fellow citizens, our way of life, our very freedom came under attack in a series of deliberate and deadly terrorist acts. The victims were in airplanes, or in their offices; secretaries, businessmen and women, military and federal workers; moms and dads, friends and neighbors. Thousands of lives were suddenly ended by evil, despicable acts of terror.

The pictures of airplanes flying into buildings, fires burning, huge structures collapsing, have filled us with disbelief, terrible sadness, and a quiet, unyielding anger. These acts of mass murder were intended to frighten our nation into chaos and retreat. But they have failed; our country is strong.

A great people has been moved to defend a great nation. Terrorist attacks can shake the foundations of our biggest buildings, but they cannot touch the foundation of America. These acts shattered steel, but they cannot dent the steel of American resolve.

America was targeted for attack because we're the brightest beacon for freedom and opportunity in the world. And no one will keep that light from shining.

Today, our nation saw evil, the very worst of human nature. And we responded with the best of America — with the daring of our rescue workers, with the caring for strangers and neighbors who came to give blood and help in any way they could.

Immediately following the first attack, I implemented our

government's emergency response plans. Our military is powerful, and it's prepared. Our emergency teams are working in New York City and Washington, D.C. to help with local rescue efforts.

Our first priority is to get help to those who have been injured, and to take every precaution to protect our citizens at home and around the world from further attacks.

The functions of our government continue without interruption. Federal agencies in Washington which had to be evacuated today are reopening for essential personnel tonight, and will be open for business tomorrow. Our financial institutions remain strong, and the American economy will be open for business, as well.

The search is underway for those who are behind these evil acts. I've directed the full resources of our intelligence and law enforcement communities to find those responsible and to bring them to justice. We will make no distinction between the terrorists who committed these acts and those who harbor them.

I appreciate so very much the members of Congress who have joined me in strongly condemning these attacks. And on behalf of the American people, I thank the many world leaders who have called to offer their condolences and assistance.

America and our friends and allies join with all those who want peace and security in the world, and we stand together to win the war against terrorism. Tonight, I ask for your prayers for all those who grieve, for the children whose worlds have been shattered, for all whose sense of safety and security has been threatened.

And I pray they will be comforted by a power greater than any of us, spoken through the ages in Psalm 23: "Even though I

walk through the valley of the shadow of death, I fear no evil,
for You are with me."

This is a day when all Americans from every walk of life unite
in our resolve for justice and peace. America has stood down
enemies before, and we will do so this time. None of us will
ever forget this day. Yet, we go forward to defend freedom and
all that is good and just in our world.

Thank you.
Good night, and God bless America."

Ken Livingstone

*On the 8th July 2005, London's Mayor responded to the
bombings in the capital the previous day – 7/7:*

"Our thoughts are with those who have been injured.

Our thoughts and efforts of the administration at City Hall
will be to care for them and to care for those who have lost
their loved ones, and there has been loss of lives.

I want to thank the emergency services for the way they've
responded.

Following the Al Qaeda attacks on Sept 11 in America, we've
conducted a series of exercises in London in order to be
prepared for such an attack.

One of those exercises, which was done by the government,
my office and the emergency and security services, was based
on the possibility of multiple explosions on the transport
system during the rush hour.

And so the plan that followed from that exercise is being followed today - with remarkable efficiency and courage, and I praise those staff who are doing that.

I'd like to thank Londoners for the calm way they've responded to this cowardly attack. Do not travel. Take the advice of the police. Stay at home.

If you're not at home, wait until you hear the advice over the radio or television from the police on how to get home later today.

I have no doubt whatsoever that this is a terrorist attack. We did hope in the first few minutes after hearing the events on the underground that it might simply be a maintenance tragedy. That was not the case.

I have been able to stay in touch by the very excellent communications that were established for the eventuality that I might be out of the city at the time of the terrorist attack, and they have worked remarkably.

And I will continue to be in touch until I board the plane that takes me back to London in the next few hours. I want to say one thing specifically to the world today.

This was not a terrorist attack against the mighty and powerful, it was not aimed at presidents or prime ministers. It was aimed at ordinary, working-class Londoners, black and white, Muslim and Christian, Hindu and Jews, young and old; an indiscriminate attempt to slaughter, irrespective of any consideration for age, for castes, for religions, whatever.

That isn't an ideology, that isn't even a perverted faith. It is just an indiscriminate attempt at mass murder. We know what the objective is. They seek to divide Londoners. They seek to turn Londoners against each other.

I said yesterday to the International Olympic Committee, this city of London is the greatest in the world because everybody lives side by side in harmony. And Londoners will not be divided by this cowardly attack.

They will stand together in solidarity around those who have been injured and those who have been bereaved. That is why I am proud to be the mayor of that city.

Finally, I wish to speak through you, directly, to those who came to London today to take lives. I do know that you do not fear to give your own lives. That is why you are so dangerous. But I do know that you fear you may fail in your long-term objective to destroy our free society.

I can show you why you'll fail. In the days that follow, look at our airports, look at our seaports, and look at our railway stations. And even after your cowardly attacks, people from the rest of Britain, people from around the world will arrive in London to become Londoners and to fulfil their dreams and achieve their potential.

They choose to come to London, as so many have come before, because they come to be free, they come to live the life they choose, they come to be able to be themselves.

They flee you, because you tell them how they should live. They don't want that. And however many of us you kill, you will not stop their flight to our cities where freedom is strong and where people can live in harmony with one another.

Whatever you do, however many you kill, you will fail."

WINSTON CHURCHILL THE GREAT WARTIME ORATOR

"I have nothing to offer but blood, toil, tears, and sweat."

Winston Churchill

Note: In compiling this book on Words of War one of the most difficult tasks has been deciding what to keep and what to omit from Churchill's World War II speeches. They were long and detailed – every word and sentence inspired the free world at its darkest hour – but too long to include them in their entirety in an anthology such as this. By retaining what I have, the intent is to set the context of each speech and include not only some of Churchill's famous statements but some of his equally powerful but lesser known words of war. (It's worth comparing Churchill's words with Adolf Hitler's speech to the Reichstag – given at the same time – see page 77–86).

"Blood, Sweat and Tears" speech delivered to the House of Commons, London – May 13th 1940:

"On Friday evening last I received from His Majesty the mission to form a new administration. It was the evident will of Parliament and the nation that this should be conceived on the broadest possible basis and that it should include all parties…

A war cabinet has been formed of five members, representing, with the Labour, Opposition, and Liberals, the unity of the nation. It was necessary that this should be done in one single day on account of the extreme urgency and rigor of events. Other key positions were filled yesterday…

I say to the House as I said to ministers who have joined this government, I have nothing to offer but blood, toil, tears, and sweat. We have before us an ordeal of the most grievous kind. We have before us many, many months of struggle and suffering.

You ask, what is our policy? I say it is to wage war by land, sea, and air. War with all our might and with all the strength God has given us, and to wage war against a monstrous tyranny never surpassed in the dark and lamentable catalogue of human crime. That is our policy.

You ask, what is our aim? I can answer in one word. It is victory. Victory at all costs - Victory in spite of all terrors - Victory, however long and hard the road may be, for without victory there is no survival.

Let that be realized. No survival for the British Empire, no survival for all that the British Empire has stood for, no survival for the urge, the impulse of the ages, that mankind shall move forward toward his goal.

I take up my task in buoyancy and hope. I feel sure that our cause will not be suffered to fail among men. I feel entitled at this juncture, at this time, to claim the aid of all and to say, "Come then, let us go forward together with our united strength."

"Fight them on the beaches" speech delivered to the House of Commons, London – 4 June 1940:

"I have, myself, full confidence that if all do their duty, if nothing is neglected, and if the best arrangements are made, as they are being made, we shall prove ourselves once again able to defend our Island home, to ride out the storm of war, and to outlive the menace of tyranny, if necessary for years, if necessary alone.

At any rate, that is what we are going to try to do. That is the resolve of His Majesty's Government-every man of them. That is the will of Parliament and the nation.

The British Empire and the French Republic, linked together in their cause and in their need, will defend to the death their native soil, aiding each other like good comrades to the utmost of their strength.

Even though large tracts of Europe and many old and famous States have fallen or may fall into the grip of the Gestapo and all the odious apparatus of Nazi rule, we shall not flag or fail.

We shall go on to the end, we shall fight in France, we shall fight on the seas and oceans, we shall fight with growing confidence and growing strength in the air, we shall defend our island, whatever the cost may be, we shall fight on the beaches, we shall fight on the landing grounds, we shall fight in the fields and in the streets, we shall fight in the hills; we shall never surrender, and even if, which I do not for a moment believe, this Island or a large part of it were subjugated and starving, then our Empire beyond the seas, armed and guarded by the British Fleet, would carry on the struggle, until, in God's good time, the New World, with all its power and might, steps forth to the rescue and the liberation of the old."

"Their Finest Hour" speech, delivered to the House of Commons, London – June 18, 1940:

"I spoke the other day of the colossal military disaster which occurred when the French High Command failed to withdraw the northern Armies from Belgium at the moment when they knew that the French front was decisively broken at Sedan and on the Meuse. This delay entailed the loss of fifteen or sixteen French divisions and threw out of action for the critical period the whole of the British Expeditionary Force. Our Army and 120,000 French troops were indeed rescued by the British Navy from Dunkirk but only with the loss of their cannon, vehicles and modern equipment.

The disastrous military events which have happened during the past fortnight have not come to me with any sense of surprise. Indeed, I indicated a fortnight ago as clearly as I could to the House that the worst possibilities were open; and I made it perfectly clear then that whatever happened in France would make no difference to the resolve of Britain and the British Empire to fight on, 'if necessary, for years, if necessary, alone.'

We have, therefore, in this Island today a very large and powerful military force. This force comprises all our best-trained and our finest troops, including scores of thousands of those who have already measured their quality against the Germans and found themselves at no disadvantage. We have under arms at the present time in this Island over a million and a quarter men...We have also over here Dominions armies. The Canadians had actually landed in France, but have now been safely withdrawn, much disappointed, but in perfect order, with all their artillery and equipment. And these very high-class forces from the Dominions will now take part in the defence of the Mother Country.

Therefore, it seems to me that as far as sea-borne invasion on a great scale is concerned, we are far more capable of meeting it today than we were at many periods in the last war and during the early months of this war ... Untiring vigilance and untiring searching of the mind is being, and must be, devoted to the subject, because, remember, the enemy is crafty and there is no dirty trick he will not do.

In the defence of this Island the advantages to the defenders will be much greater than they were in the fighting around Dunkirk. I look forward confidently to the exploits of our fighter pilots – these splendid men, this brilliant youth – who will have the glory of saving their native land, their island home, and all they love, from the most deadly of all attacks.

There remains, of course, the danger of bombing attacks, which will certainly be made very soon upon us by the bomber forces of the enemy. It is true that the German bomber force is superior in numbers to ours; but we have a very large bomber force also, which we shall use to strike at military targets in Germany without intermission. I do not at all underrate the severity of the ordeal which lies before us; but I believe our

countrymen will show themselves capable of standing up to it,
I have thought it right upon this occasion to give the House
and the country some indication of the solid, practical grounds
upon which we base our inflexible resolve to continue the war.
There are a good many people who say, "Never mind. Win or
lose, sink or swim, better die than submit to tyranny – and
such a tyranny." And I do not dissociate myself from them.
But I can assure them that our professional advisers of the
three Services unitedly advise that we should carry on the war,
and that there are good and reasonable hopes of final victory.
We have fully informed and consulted all the self-governing
Dominions, these great communities far beyond the oceans
who have been built up on our laws and on our civilization,
and who are absolutely free to choose their course, but are
absolutely devoted to the ancient Motherland, and who feel
themselves inspired by the same emotions which lead me to
stake our all upon duty and honour. We have fully consulted
them ... They endorse our decision to fight on, and declare
themselves ready to share our fortunes and to persevere to the
end. That is what we are going to do.

If Hitler can bring under his despotic control the industries of
the countries he has conquered, this will add greatly to his
already vast armament output. On the other hand, this will not
happen immediately, and we are now assured of immense,
continuous and increasing support in supplies and munitions
of all kinds from the United States; and especially of
aeroplanes and pilots from the Dominions and across the
oceans coming from regions which are beyond the reach of
enemy bombers.

I do not see how any of these factors can operate to our
detriment on balance before the winter comes; and the winter
will impose a strain upon the Nazi regime, with almost all
Europe writhing and starving under its cruel heel, which, for
all their ruthlessness, will run them very hard. We must not
forget that from the moment when we declared war on the 3rd

September it was always possible for Germany to turn all her Air Force upon this country, together with any other devices of invasion she might conceive, and that France could have done little or nothing to prevent her doing so. We have, therefore, lived under this danger, in principle and in a slightly modified form, during all these months. In the meanwhile, however, we have enormously improved our methods of defence...

What General Weygand called the Battle of France is over. I expect that the Battle of Britain is about to begin. Upon this battle depends the survival of Christian civilization. Upon it depends our own British life, and the long continuity of our institutions and our Empire. The whole fury and might of the enemy must very soon be turned on us. Hitler knows that he will have to break us in this Island or lose the war. If we can stand up to him, all Europe may be free and the life of the world may move forward into broad, sunlit uplands. But if we fail, then the whole world, including the United States, including all that we have known and cared for, will sink into the abyss of a new Dark Age made more sinister, and perhaps more protracted, by the lights of perverted science. Let us therefore brace ourselves to our duties, and so bear ourselves that, if the British Empire and its Commonwealth last for a thousand years, men will still say, 'This was their finest hour'."

"The Few" speech, delivered to the House of Commons, London – August 20, 1940:

"Almost a year has passed since the war began, and it is natural for us, I think, to pause on our journey at this milestone and survey the dark, wide field. It is also useful to compare the first year of this second war against German aggression with its forerunner a quarter of a century ago. Although this war is in fact only a continuation of the last, very great differences in its character are apparent. In the last war millions of men fought by hurling enormous masses of steel at one another. "Men and shells" was the cry, and prodigious slaughter was the consequence.

In this war nothing of this kind has yet appeared. It is a conflict of strategy, of organization, of technical apparatus, of science, mechanics, and morale. The British casualties in the first 12 months of the Great War amounted to 365,000. In this war, I am thankful to say, British killed, wounded, prisoners, and missing, including civilians, do not exceed 92,000, and of these a large proportion are alive as prisoners of war. Looking more widely around, one may say that throughout all Europe for one man killed or wounded in the first year perhaps five were killed or wounded in 1914-15.

The slaughter is only a small fraction, but the consequences to the belligerents have been even more deadly. We have seen great countries with powerful armies dashed out of coherent existence in a few weeks...

There is another more obvious difference from 1914. The whole of the warring nations are engaged, not only soldiers, but the entire population, men, women, and children. The fronts are everywhere. The trenches are dug in the towns and streets. Every village is fortified. Every road is barred. The front line runs through the factories. The workmen are soldiers with different weapons but the same courage. These are great and distinctive changes from what many of us saw in the struggle of a quarter of a century ago.

There seems to be every reason to believe that this new kind of war is well suited to the genius and the resources of the British nation and the British Empire and that, once we get properly equipped and properly started, a war of this kind will be more favourable to us than the sombre mass slaughters of the Somme and Passchendaele. If it is a case of the whole nation fighting and suffering together, that ought to suit us, because we are the most united of all the nations, because we entered the war upon the national will and with our eyes open, and because we have been nurtured in freedom and individual responsibility and are the products, not of totalitarian uniformity but of tolerance and variety.

If all these qualities are turned, as they are being turned, to the arts of war, we may be able to show the enemy quite a lot of things that they have not thought of yet. Since the Germans drove the Jews out and lowered their technical standards, our science is definitely ahead of theirs. Our geographical position, the command of the sea, and the friendship of the United States enable us to draw resources from the whole world and to manufacture weapons of war of every kind, but especially of the superfine kinds, on a scale hitherto practised only by Nazi Germany.

Hitler is now sprawled over Europe. Our offensive springs are being slowly compressed, and we must resolutely and methodically prepare ourselves for the campaigns of 1941 and 1942...

One of the ways to bring this war to a speedy end is to convince the enemy, not by words, but by deeds, that we have both the will and the means, not only to go on indefinitely but to strike heavy and unexpected blows. The road to victory may not be so long as we expect. But we have no right to count upon this. Be it long or short, rough or smooth, we mean to reach our journey's end...

Let Hitler bear his responsibilities to the full and let the peoples of Europe who groan beneath his yoke aid in every way the coming of the day when that yoke will be broken...

Rather more than a quarter of a year has passed since the new Government came into power in this country. What a cataract of disaster has poured out upon us since then. The trustful Dutch overwhelmed; their beloved and respected Sovereign driven into exile; the peaceful city of Rotterdam the scene of a massacre as hideous and brutal as anything in the Thirty Years' War. Belgium invaded and beaten down; our own fine Expeditionary Force, which King Leopold called to his rescue, cut off and almost captured, escaping as it seemed only by a miracle and with the loss of all its equipment; our Ally, France, out; Italy in against us; all France in the power of the enemy, all its arsenals and vast masses of military material converted or convertible to the enemy's use; a puppet Government set up at Vichy which may at any moment be forced to become our foe; the whole Western seaboard of Europe from the North Cape to the Spanish frontier in German hands; all the ports, all the air-fields on this immense front, employed against us as potential springboards of invasion. Moreover, the German air power, numerically so far outstripping ours, has been brought so close to our Island that what we used to dread greatly has come to pass and the hostile bombers not only reach our shores in a few minutes and from many directions, but can be escorted by their fighting aircraft.

Let us see what has happened on the other side of the scales. The British nation and the British Empire, finding themselves alone, stood undismayed against disaster. No one flinched or wavered; nay, some who formerly thought of peace, now think only of war. Our people are united and resolved, as they have never been before. Death and ruin have become small things compared with the shame of defeat or failure in duty.

We cannot tell what lies ahead. It may be that even greater ordeals lie before us. We shall face whatever is coming to us. We are sure of ourselves and of our cause and that is the supreme fact which has emerged in these months of trial.

Meanwhile, we have not only fortified our hearts but our Island. We have rearmed and rebuilt our armies in a degree which would have been deemed impossible a few months ago... More than 2,000,000 determined men have rifles and bayonets in their hands to-night and three-quarters of them are in regular military formations. We have never had armies like this in our Island in time of war. The whole Island bristles against invaders, from the sea or from the air...

Our Navy is far stronger than it was at the beginning of the war. The great flow of new construction set on foot at the outbreak is now beginning to come in. We hope our friends across the ocean will send us a timely reinforcement to bridge the gap between the peace flotillas of 1939 and the war flotillas of 1941. There is no difficulty in sending such aid. The seas and oceans are open. The U-boats are contained...

Why do I say all this? Not assuredly to boast; not assuredly to give the slightest countenance to complacency. The dangers we face are still enormous, but so are our advantages and resources.

I recount them because the people have a right to know that there are solid grounds for the confidence which we feel, and that we have good reason to believe ourselves capable, as I said in a very dark hour two months ago, of continuing the war "if necessary alone, if necessary for years." I say it also because the fact that the British Empire stands invincible, and that Nazidom is still being resisted, will kindle again the spark of hope in the breasts of hundreds of millions of downtrodden or despairing men and women throughout Europe, and far beyond its bounds, and that from these sparks there will presently come cleansing and devouring flame.

The great air battle which has been in progress over this Island for the last few weeks has recently attained a high intensity. It is too soon to attempt to assign limits either to its scale or to its duration. We must certainly expect that greater efforts will be made by the enemy than any he has so far put forth. Hostile air fields are still being developed in France and the Low Countries, and the movement of squadrons and material for attacking us is still proceeding.

It is quite plain that Herr Hitler could not admit defeat in his air attack on Great Britain without sustaining most serious injury. If, after all his boastings and blood-curdling threats and lurid accounts trumpeted round the world of the damage he has inflicted, of the vast numbers of our Air Force he has shot down, so he says, with so little loss to himself; if after tales of the panic-stricken British crushed in their holes cursing the plutocratic Parliament which has led them to such a plight; if after all this his whole air onslaught were forced after a while tamely to peter out, the Fuehrer's reputation for veracity of statement might be seriously impugned. We may be sure, therefore, that he will continue as long as he has the strength to do so, and as long as any preoccupations he may have in respect of the Russian Air Force allow him to do so...

The enemy is, of course, far more numerous than we are. But our new production already, as I am advised, largely exceeds his...

The gratitude of every home in our Island, in our Empire, and indeed throughout the world, except in the abodes of the guilty, goes out to the British airmen who, undaunted by odds, unwearied in their constant challenge and mortal danger, are turning the tide of the world war by their prowess and by their devotion. Never in the field of human conflict was so much owed by so many to so few...

All hearts go out to the fighter pilots, whose brilliant actions we see with our own eyes day after day; but we must never forget that all the time, night after night, month after month, our bomber squadrons travel far into Germany, find their targets in the darkness by the highest navigational skill, aim their attacks, often under the heaviest fire, often with serious loss, with deliberate careful discrimination, and inflict shattering blows upon the whole of the technical and war-making structure of the Nazi power...

Undoubtedly this process means that these two great organizations of the English-speaking democracies, the British Empire and the United States, will have to be somewhat mixed up together in some of their affairs for mutual and general advantage.

For my own part, looking out upon the future, I do not view the process with any misgivings. I could not stop it if I wished; no one can stop it. Like the Mississippi, it just keeps rolling along. Let it roll. Let it roll on full flood, inexorable, irresistible, benignant, to broader lands and better days."

"Never Give In" speech, delivered at Harrow School, London – October 29, 1941:

"Almost a year has passed since I came down here at your Head Master's kind invitation in order to cheer myself and cheer the hearts of a few of my friends by singing some of our own songs.

The ten months that have passed have seen very terrible catastrophic events in the world - ups and downs, misfortunes - but can anyone sitting here this afternoon, this October afternoon, not feel deeply thankful for what has happened in the time that has passed and for the very great improvement in the position of our country and of our home? Why, when I was here last time we were quite alone, desperately alone, and we had been so for five or six months. We were poorly armed. We are not so poorly armed today; but then we were very poorly armed. We had the unmeasured menace of the enemy and their air attack still beating upon us, and you yourselves had had experience of this attack; and I expect you are beginning to feel impatient that there has been this long lull with nothing particular turning up!

But we must learn to be equally good at what is short and sharp and what is long and tough. It is generally said that the British are often better at the last. They do not expect to move from crisis to crisis; they do not always expect that each day will bring up some noble chance of war; but when they very slowly make up their minds that the thing has to be done and the job put through and finished, then, even if it takes months - if it takes years - they do it.

Another lesson I think we may take, just throwing our minds back to our meeting here ten months ago and now, is that appearances are often very deceptive, and as Kipling well says, we must "...meet with Triumph and Disaster. And treat those two impostors just the same."

You cannot tell from appearances how things will go. Sometimes imagination makes things out far worse than they are; yet without imagination not much can be done. Those people who are imaginative see many more dangers than perhaps exist; certainly many more than will happen; but then they must also pray to be given that extra courage to carry this far-reaching imagination. But for everyone, surely, what we have gone through in this period - I am addressing myself to the School - surely from this period of ten months this is the lesson: never give in, never give in, never, never, never, never – in nothing, great or small, large or petty – never give in except to convictions of honour and good sense. Never yield to force; never yield to the apparently overwhelming might of the enemy. We stood all alone a year ago, and to many countries it seemed that our account was closed, we were finished. All this tradition of ours, our songs, our School history, this part of the history of this country, were gone and finished and liquidated.

Very different is the mood today. Britain, other nations thought, had drawn a sponge across her slate. But instead our country stood in the gap. There was no flinching and no thought of giving in; and by what seemed almost a miracle to those outside these Islands, though we ourselves never doubted it, we now find ourselves in a position where I say that we can be sure that we have only to persevere to conquer.

You sang here a verse of a School Song: you sang that extra verse written in my honour, which I was very greatly complimented by and which you have repeated today. But there is one word in it I want to alter - I wanted to do so last year, but I did not venture to. It is the line: "Not less we praise in darker days."

I have obtained the Head Master's permission to alter darker to sterner. "Not less we praise in sterner days."

Do not let us speak of darker days: let us speak rather of sterner days. These are not dark days; these are great days - the greatest days our country has ever lived; and we must all thank God that we have been allowed, each of us according to our stations, to play a part in making these days memorable in the history of our race."

WISE WORDS THOUGHTS AND COMMENTS ON WARFARE

"Being unconquerable lies with yourself;
being conquerable lies with your enemy."

Sun Tzu

Sun Tzu

Sun Tzu (544–496BC) was a Chinese military strategist. His writings on "The Art of War" have had a considerable impact on Western military (and business) thinking and still do today.

"All men can see these tactics whereby I conquer, but what none can see is the strategy out of which victory is evolved."

"All war is based on deception."

"Be extremely subtle, even to the point of formlessness. Be extremely mysterious, even to the point of soundlessness. Thereby you can be the director of the opponent's fate."

"For to win one hundred victories in one hundred battles is not the acme of skill. To subdue the enemy without fighting is the acme of skill."

"He who knows when he can fight and when he cannot, will be victorious."

"Hence that general is skilful in attack whose opponent does not know what to defend; and he is skilful in defence whose opponent does not know what to attack."

"If ignorant both of your enemy and yourself, you are certain to be in peril."

"If you are far from the enemy, make him believe you are near."

"If you know the enemy and know yourself you need not fear the results of a hundred battles."

"In the practical art of war, the best thing of all is to take the enemy's country whole and intact; to shatter and destroy it is not so good."

"It is essential to seek out enemy agents who have come to conduct espionage against you and to bribe them to serve you. Give them instructions and care for them. Thus double agents are recruited and used."

"The reason the enlightened prince and the wise general conquer the enemy whenever they move and their achievements surpass those of ordinary men is foreknowledge."

"Regard your soldiers as your children, and they will follow you into the deepest valleys; look on them as your own beloved sons, and they will stand by you even unto death."

"Secret operations are essential in war; upon them the army relies to make its every move."

"The general who advances without coveting fame and retreats without fearing disgrace, whose only thought is to protect his country and do good service for his sovereign, is the jewel of the kingdom."

"The opportunity to secure ourselves against defeat lies in our own hands, but the opportunity of defeating the enemy is provided by the enemy himself."

"The quality of decision is like the well-timed swoop of a falcon which enables it to strike and destroy its victim."

"The skilful employer of men will employ the wise man, the brave man, the covetous man, and the stupid man."

"There has never been a protracted war from which a country has benefited."

Aristotle

Greek philosopher (384BC–322), student of Plato and tutor to Alexander the Great

"Those who cannot bravely face danger are the slaves of their attackers."

Alexander the Great

King of Macedon (336BC-323BC) – on taking charge of an attack on a fortress.

"There is nothing impossible to him who will try."

"I would not fear a pack of lions led by a sheep, but I would always fear a flock of sheep led by a lion."

Emperor Charlemagne

Founder of the Carolingian Empire, reigning from 768 to814

"Quamvis enim melius sit benefacere quam nosse,
prius tamen est nosse quam facere."
(*"Right action is better than knowledge; but in order to do what is right, we must know what is right."*)

Genghis Khan

He united many of the tribes of NE Asia and founded the great Mongol empire, which he ruled 1206–1227:

"One arrow alone can be easily broken but many arrows are indestructible."

"The greatest happiness is to vanquish your enemies, to drive them before you, to see his cities reduced to ashes, to see those who love him bathed in tears, to clasp to your bosom his wives and daughters."

Oliver Cromwell

Letter to Sir William Spring (September 1643):

"I had rather have a plain, russet-coated Captain, that knows what he fights for, and loves what he knows, than that you call a Gentleman and is nothing else."

Napoleon Bonaparte

French military and political leader 1769–1821:

"The battlefield is a scene of constant chaos. The winner will be the one who controls that chaos, both his own and the enemy's."

"One must change one's tactics every ten years if one wishes to maintain one's superiority."

"Never interrupt your enemy when he is making a mistake."

"The most important qualification of a soldier is fortitude under fatigue and privation. Courage is only second; hardship, poverty and want are the best school for a soldier."

"He who fears being conquered is certain of defeat."

Robert E. Lee

American Civil War Commander of the Confederate Army of North Virginia:

"It is good that war is so horrible, or we might grow to like it."

"A true man of honour feels humbled himself when he cannot help humbling others."

"Duty is the most sublime word in our language. Do your duty in all things. You cannot do more. You should never wish to do less."

"I cannot trust a man to control others who cannot control himself."

"I have been up to see the Congress and they do not seem to be able to do anything except to eat peanuts and chew tobacco, while my army is starving."

"I think it better to do right, even if we suffer in so doing, than to incur the reproach of our consciences and posterity."

"The war... was an unnecessary condition of affairs, and might have been avoided if forbearance and wisdom had been practiced on both sides."

"We have fought this fight as long, and as well as we know how. We have been defeated. For us as a Christian people, there is now but one course to pursue. We must accept the situation."

"We must expect reverses, even defeats. They are sent to teach us wisdom and prudence, to call forth greater energies, and to prevent our falling into greater disasters."

"What a cruel thing war is... to fill our hearts with hatred instead of love for our neighbours."

William Tecumseh Sherman

Union general – American Civil War (1861–1865):

"A battery of field artillery is worth a thousand muskets."

"Every attempt to make war easy and safe will result in humiliation and disaster."

"I hate newspapermen. They come into camp and pick up their camp rumors and print them as facts. I regard them as spies, which, in truth, they are."

"I intend to make Georgia howl."

"I would make this war as severe as possible, and show no symptoms of tiring till the South begs for mercy."

"War is the remedy that our enemies have chosen, and I say let us give them all they want."

"War is too serious a matter to leave to soldiers."

"War is hell."

Carl von Clausewitz

Prussian (and for a while Russian) soldier and military theorist – best known for his seminal and still read book 'Vom Kriege' ('On War') which was unfinished on his death in 1831 but was posthumously published by his wife in several volumes between 1832 and 1835:

"War is not an independent phenomenon, but the continuation of politics by different means."

"A conqueror is always a lover of peace."

"All action takes place, so to speak, in a kind of twilight, which like a fog or moonlight, often tends to make things seem grotesque and larger than they really are."

"Although our intellect always longs for clarity and certainty, our nature often finds uncertainty fascinating."

"Courage, above all things, is the first quality of a warrior."

"Everything in war is very simple.
But the simplest thing is difficult."

"I shall proceed from the simple to the complex. But in war more than in any other subject we must begin by looking at the nature of the whole; for here more than elsewhere the part and the whole must always be thought of together."

"If the leader is filled with high ambition and if he pursues his aims with audacity and strength of will, he will reach them in spite of all obstacles."

"It is even better to act quickly and err than to hesitate until the time of action is past."

"Many intelligence reports in war are contradictory; even more are false, and most are uncertain."

"Never forget that no military leader has ever become great without audacity."

"Politics is the womb in which war develops."

"Pursue one great decisive aim with force and determination."

"The backbone of surprise is fusing speed with secrecy."

"The more a general is accustomed to place heavy demands on his soldiers, the more he can depend on their response."

"The political object is the goal, war is the means of reaching it, and the means can never be considered in isolation from their purposes."

"To secure peace is to prepare for war."

"Two qualities are indispensable: first, an intellect that, even in the darkest hour, retains some glimmerings of the inner light which leads to truth; and second, the courage to follow this faint light wherever it may lead."

"War is not an exercise of the will directed at an inanimate matter."

Ulysses S. Grant

Union General – American Civil War:

"Although a soldier by profession, I have never felt any sort of fondness for war, and I have never advocated it, except as a means of peace."

General Douglas MacArthur

US General who rose to prominence during World War II and subsequently commanded the United Troops during the Korean War.

"It is fatal to enter any war without the will to win it."

"A general is just as good or just as bad as the troops under his command make him."

"Never give an order that can't be obeyed."

"The best luck of all is the luck you make for yourself."

"Build me a son, O Lord, who will be strong enough to know when he is weak, and brave enough to face himself when he is afraid, one who will be proud and unbending in honest defeat, and humble and gentle in victory."

"Duty, Honour, Country. Those three hallowed words reverently dictate what you ought to be, what you can be, what you will be."

"I have known war as few men now living know it. Its very destructiveness on both friend and foe has rendered it useless as a means of settling international disputes."

"In war there is no substitute for victory."

"Could I have but a line a century hence crediting a contribution to the advance of peace, I would yield every honour which has been accorded by war."

G.K. Chesterton

English writer (1874–1936)

"The true soldier fights not because he hates what is in front of him, but because he loves what is behind him."

General Dwight D. Eisenhower

In 1942 Eisenhower was appointed Supreme Allied Commander in North Africa and Europe. After the War he became 34th US President from 1953 to 1961.

"I hate war as only a soldier who has lived it can, only as one who has seen its brutality, its stupidity."

"Leadership is the art of getting someone else to do something you want done because he wants to do it."

"Neither a wise nor a brave man lies down on the tracks of history to wait for the train of the future to run over him."

"The best morale exists when you never hear the word mentioned. When you hear it it's usually lousy."

"In preparing for battle I have always found that plans are useless, but planning is indispensable."

"Only our individual faith in freedom can keep us free."

General George Patton

World War II US General (1885–1945):

"Better to fight for something than live for nothing."

"My men don't surrender. I don't want to hear of any soldier under my command being captured unless he has been hit. Even if you are hit, you can still fight back."

"A good plan violently executed now is better than a perfect plan executed next week."

"Accept the challenges so that you can feel the exhilaration of victory. "

"All very successful commanders are prima donnas and must be so treated. "

"Battle is the most magnificent competition in which a human being can indulge. It brings out all that is best; it removes all that is base. All men are afraid in battle. The coward is the one who lets his fear overcome his sense of duty. Duty is the essence of manhood."

"Courage is fear holding on a minute longer."

"I don't measure a man's success by how high he climbs but how high he bounces when he hits bottom."

"If everyone is thinking alike, then somebody isn't thinking."

"If we take the generally accepted definition of bravery as a quality which knows no fear, I have never seen a brave man. All men are frightened. The more intelligent they are, the more they are frightened."

"If you tell people where to go, but not how to get there, you'll be amazed at the results."

"The time to take counsel of your fears is before you make an important battle decision. That's the time to listen to every fear you can imagine! When you have collected all the facts and fears and made your decision, turn off all your fears and go ahead!"

"Untutored courage is useless in the face of educated bullets."

"We herd sheep, we drive cattle, we lead people. Lead me, follow me, or get out of my way."

Albert Einstein

German-born theoretical physicist (1879–1955)

"I know not with what weapons World War III will be fought, but World War IV will be fought with sticks and stones."

THE PEN IS MIGHTIER THAN THE SWORD
WARLIKE WORDS FROM FICTION

"I am never going to have anything more to do with politics or politicians. When this war is over I shall confine myself entirely to writing and painting."

Winston Churchill

Maximus

In the film Gladiator (2000)

"At my signal, unleash hell."

William Shakespeare

Julius Caesar (C.1599)
(Act 3 scene 1)
Mark Antony – seeking revenge on the death of Caesar

"And Caesar's spirit, raging for revenge,
With Ate by his side come hot from hell,
Shall in these confines with a monarch's voice
Cry "Havoc!" and let slip the dogs of war,
That this foul deed shall smell above the earth
With carrion men, groaning for burial."

Henry V (c.1599) – Siege of Harfleur
(Act 3 Scene 1)
King Henry V:

"Once more unto the breach, dear friends, once more;
Or close the wall up with our English dead.
In peace there's nothing so becomes a man
As modest stillness and humility:
But when the blast of war blows in our ears,
Then imitate the action of the tiger;
Stiffen the sinews, summon up the blood,
Disguise fair nature with hard-favour'd rage;
Then lend the eye a terrible aspect;
Let pry through the portage of the head

Like the brass cannon; let the brow o'erwhelm it
As fearfully as doth a galled rock
O'erhang and jutty his confounded base,
Swill'd with the wild and wasteful ocean.
Now set the teeth and stretch the nostril wide,
Hold hard the breath and bend up every spirit
To his full height. On, on, you noblest English.
Whose blood is fet from fathers of war-proof!
Fathers that, like so many Alexanders,
Have in these parts from morn till even fought
And sheathed their swords for lack of argument:
Dishonour not your mothers; now attest
That those whom you call'd fathers did beget you.
Be copy now to men of grosser blood,
And teach them how to war. And you, good yeoman,
Whose limbs were made in England, show us here
The mettle of your pasture; let us swear
That you are worth your breeding; which I doubt not;
For there is none of you so mean and base,
That hath not noble lustre in your eyes.
I see you stand like greyhounds in the slips,
Straining upon the start. The game's afoot:
Follow your spirit, and upon this charge
Cry 'God for Harry, England, and Saint George!'"

Henry V
(Act 4 Scene 3)
Westmoreland:

"O that we now had here
But one ten thousand of those men in England
That do no work to-day!"

King:
"What's he that wishes so?
My cousin Westmoreland? No, my fair cousin;

If we are mark'd to die, we are enow
To do our country loss; and if to live,
The fewer men, the greater share of honour.
God's will! I pray thee, wish not one man more...

Rather proclaim it, Westmoreland, through my host,
That he which hath no stomach to this fight,
Let him depart; his passport shall be made,
And crowns for convoy put into his purse;
We would not die in that man's company
That fears his fellowship to die with us.
This day is call'd the feast of Crispian.
He that outlives this day, and comes safe home,
Will stand a tip-toe when this day is nam'd,
And rouse him at the name of Crispian.
He that shall live this day, and see old age,
Will yearly on the vigil feast his neighbours,
And say 'To-morrow is Saint Crispian.'
Then will he strip his sleeve and show his scars,
And say 'These wounds I had on Crispin's day.'
Old men forget; yet all shall be forgot,
But he'll remember, with advantages...

This story shall the good man teach his son;
And Crispin Crispian shall ne'er go by,
From this day to the ending of the world,
But we in it shall be remembered-
We few, we happy few, we band of brothers;
For he to-day that sheds his blood with me
Shall be my brother; be he ne'er so vile,
This day shall gentle his condition;
And gentlemen in England now a-bed
Shall think themselves accurs'd they were not here,
And hold their manhoods cheap whiles any speaks
That fought with us upon Saint Crispin's day."

Thomas Babington Macaulay, Lord Macaulay

Lars Porsena, an Etruscan King, led a revolution against Rome in 508BC. There are various stories of Roman bravery defending his assault on the city, of which Macaulay's Horatius (1842) (from the poet's set of narrative poems - Lays of Ancient Rome) is just one. The following are a selection of verses from the poem's seventy.

The intent is to capture the spirit of this epic defence of the bridge into Rome by Horatius and the two who "stood by him". As a delaying tactic the three Romans held off every assault on the bridge while it was being destroyed under their feet to deny the enemy entry.

XIX

They held a council standing,
Before the River-Gate;
Short time was there, ye well may guess,
For musing or debate.
Out spake the Consul roundly:
'The bridge must straight go down;
For, since Janiculum is lost,
Nought else can save the town.'

XX

Just then a scout came flying,
All wild with haste and fear:
'To arms! to arms! Sir Consul:
Lars Porsena is here.'
On the lows hills to westward
The Consul fixed his eye,
And saw the swarthy storm of dust
Rise fast along the sky.

XXII

And plainly and more plainly,
Above that glimmering line,
Now might ye see the banners
Of twelve fair cities shine;
But the banner of proud Clusium
Was highest of them all,
The terror of the Umbrian,
The terror of the Gaul.

XXVI

But the Consul's brow was sad,
And the Consul's speech was low,
And darkly looked he at the wall,
And darkly at the foe.
'Their van will be upon us
Before the bridge goes down;
And if they once may win the bridge,
What hope to save the town?'

XXVII

Then out spake brave Horatius,
The Captain of the gate:
'To every man upon this earth
Death cometh soon or late.
And how can man die better
Than facing fearful odds,
For the ashes of his fathers,
And the temples of his Gods,

XXIX

'Hew down the bridge, Sir Consul,
With all the speed ye may;
I, with two more to help me,
Will hold the foe in play.
In yon strait path a thousand
May well be stopped by three.

Now who will stand on either hand,
    And keep the bridge with me?'

XXX

Then out spake Spurius Lartius;
    A Ramnian proud was he:
'Lo, I will stand at thy right hand,
    And keep the bridge with thee.'
And out spake strong Herminius;
    Of Titian blood was he:
'I will abide on thy left side,
    And keep the bridge with thee.'

XXXI

'Horatius,' quoth the Consul,
    'As thou sayest, so let it be.'
And straight against that great array
    Forth went the dauntless Three.
For Romans in Rome's quarrel
    Spared neither land nor gold,
Nor son nor wife, nor limb nor life,
    In the brave days of old.

XXXIV

Now while the Three were tightening
    Their harness on their backs,
The Consul was the foremost man
    To take in hand an axe:
And Fathers mixed with Commons
    Seized hatchet, bar, and crow,
And smote upon the planks above,
    And loosed the props below.

XXXVI

The Three stood calm and silent,
And looked upon the foes,
And a great shout of laughter
From all the vanguard rose:
And forth three chiefs came spurring
Before that deep array;
To earth they sprang, their swords they drew,
And lifted high their shields, and flew
To win the narrow way;

XL

Herminius smote down Aruns:
Lartius laid Ocnus low:
Right to the heart of Lausulus
Horatius sent a blow.
'Lie there,' he cried, 'fell pirate!
No more, aghast and pale,
From Ostia's walls the crowd shall mark
The track of thy destroying bark.
No more Campania's hinds shall fly
To woods and caverns when they spy
Thy thrice accursed sail.'

XLII

But hark! the cry is Astur:
And lo! the ranks divide;
And the great Lord of Luna
Comes with his stately stride.
Upon his ample shoulders
Clangs loud the four-fold shield,
And in his hand he shakes the brand
Which none but he can wield.

XLIV

Then, whirling up his broadsword
With both hands to the heights
He rushed against Horatius,
And smote with all his might,
With shield and blade Horatius
Right deftly turned the blow.
The blow, though turned, came yet too nigh;
It missed his helm, but gashed his thigh:
The Tuscans raised a joyful cry
To see the red blood flow.

XLVII

On Astur's throat Horatius
Right firmly pressed his heel,
And thrice and four times tugged amain,
Ere he wrenched out the steel.
'And see,' he cried, 'the welcome,
Fair guests, that waits you here!
What noble Lucumo comes next
To taste our Roman cheer?'

XLIX

But all Etruria's noblest
Felt their hearts sink to see
On the earth the bloody corpses,
In the path the dauntless Three:
And, from the ghastly entrance
Where those bold Romans stood,
All shrank, like boys who unaware,
Ranging the woods to start a hare,
Come to the mouth of the dark lair
Where, growling low, a fierce old bear
Lies amidst bones and blood.

L

Was none who would be foremost
To lead such dire attack:
But those behind cried 'Forward!'
And those before cried 'Back!'
And backward now and forward
Wavers the deep array;
And on the tossing sea of steel,
To and fro the standards reel;
And the victorious trumpet-peal
Dies fitfully away.

LIII

But meanwhile axe and lever
Have manfully been plied;
And now the bridge hangs tottering
Above the boiling tide.
'Come back, come back, Horatius!'
Loud cried the Fathers all.
'Back, Lartius! back, Herminius!
Back, ere the ruin fall!'

LIV

Back darted Spurius Lartius;
Herminius darted back:
And, as they passed, beneath their feet
They felt the timbers crack.
But when they turned their faces,
And on the farther shore
Saw brave Horatius stand alone,
They would have crossed once more.

LV

But with a crash like thunder
Fell every loosened beam,
And, like a dam, the mighty wreck
Lay right athwart the stream:
And a long shout of triumph
Rose from the walls of Rome,
As to the highest turret-tops
Was splashed the yellow foam.

LVII

Alone stood brave Horatius,
But constant still in mind;
Thrice thirty thousand foes before,
And the broad flood behind.
'Down with him!' cried false Sextus,
With a smile on his pale face.
'Now yield thee,' cried Lars Porsena,
'Now yield thee to our grace!'

LIX

'Oh, Tiber! father Tiber!
To whom the Romans pray,
A Roman's life, a Roman's arms,
Take thou in charge this day!'
So he spake, and speaking sheathed
The good sword by his side,
And with his harness on his back,
Plunged headlong in the tide.

LX

No sound of joy or sorrow
Was heard from either bank;
But friends and foes in dumb surprise,
With parted lips and straining eyes,
Stood gazing where he sank;
And when above the surges
They saw his crest appear,
All Rome sent forth a rapturous cry,
And even the ranks of Tuscany
Could scarce forbear to cheer.

LXI

But fiercely ran the current,
Swollen high by months of rain:
And fast his blood was flowing;
And he was sore in pain,
And heavy with his armour,
And spent with changing blows:
And oft they thought him sinking,
But still again he rose.

LXIII

'Curse on him!' quoth false Sextus;
'Will not the villain drown?
But for this stay, ere close of day
We should have sacked the town!'
'Heaven help him!' quoth Lars Porsena,
'And bring him safe to shore;
For such a gallant feat of arms
Was never seen before.'

LXIV

And now he feels the bottom;
Now on dry earth he stands;
Now round him throng the Fathers;
To press his gory hands;
And now, with shouts and clapping,
And noise of weeping loud,
He enters through the River-Gate,
Borne by the joyous crowd.

LXX

When the goodman mends his armour,
And trims his helmet's plume;
When the goodwife's shuttle merrily
Goes flashing through the loom;
With weeping and with laughter
Still is the story told,
How well Horatius kept the bridge
In the brave days of old.

Alexandre Dumas

The Three Musketeers (1844)

"Never Fear quarrels, but seek hazardous adventures"

"And now gentlemen, all for one, one for all – that is our motto, is it not?"

Count Leo Tolstoy

War and Peace (1869)

"If every one fought for their own convictions there would be no war."

T.E. Lawrence

Perhaps better known as 'Lawrence of Arabia", he led the Arab Revolt against the Turkish rule (1916–1918). The Seven Pillars of Wisdom *is his autobiographical account of his wartime experiences.*

"Feisal asked me if I would wear Arab clothes like his own while in the camp. I should find it better for my own part, since it was a comfortable dress in which to live Arab-fashion as we must do. Besides, the tribesmen would then understand how to take me. The only wearers of khaki in their experience had been Turkish officers, before whom they took up an instinctive defence. If I wore Meccan clothes, they would behave to me as though I were really one of the leaders; and I might slip in and out of Feisal's tent without making a sensation which he had to explain away each time to strangers. I agreed at once, very gladly; for army uniform was abominable when camel-riding or when sitting about on the ground; and the Arab things, which I had learned to manage before the war, were cleaner and more decent in the desert."

"Irregular war was far more intellectual than a bayonet charge, far more exhausting than service in the comfortable imitative obedience of an ordered army. Guerrillas must be allowed liberal workroom: in irregular war, of two men together, one was being wasted. Our ideal should be to make our battle a series of single combats, our ranks a happy alliance of agile commanders-in-chief."

George Orwell

Homage to Catalonia (1938) shows a different, less glorious side to the war:

"One of the most horrible features of war is that all the war-propaganda, all the screaming and lies and hatred, comes invariably from people who are not fighting."

"Every war suffers a kind of progressive degradation with every month that it continues, because such things as individual liberty and a truthful press are simply not compatible with military efficiency."

"In the barn where we waited the floor was a thin layer of chaff over deep beds of bones, human bones and cows' bones mixed up, and the place was alive with rats. The filthy brutes came swarming out of the ground on every side. If there is one thing I hate more than another it is a rat running over me in the darkness."

"No one I met at this time -- doctors, nurses, practicantes, or fellow-patients -- failed to assure me that a man who is hit through the neck and survives it is the luckiest creature alive. I could not help thinking that it would be even luckier not to be hit at all."

Angelos Sikelianos

*Kostís Palam·s was Greece's leading early 20th century poet. A
champion of the everyday spoken language, he wrote the hymn
that is sung at the start of every Olympic Games. He died
during the German occupation of Greece in World War II.
His friend Angelos Sikelianos composed and recited this poem
at his burial in Athens on February 28th 1943, in defiance of
the authorities. The large crowd of mourners then sang the
(banned) national anthem. The funeral of Palamás was a
turning point in popular resistance to the hated Nazi regime.*

Sound, trumpets! Thundering bells,
shake the land bodily, end to end!
Roar, drums of war! Fearsome
banners, unfurl in the wind!

On this coffin rests Greece! A mountain
of laurels, piled up to the peaks of Pelion and Ossa,
or built like a tower to the seventh heaven,
could not enclose him, and what can my tongue say?

But you, the People, whose poor speech
this Hero took and raised to the stars,
share now the godlike radiance
of his perfect glory, lift him in your arms,

a giant pennant, and shout to the sky
with hearts aflame
in a single breath, 'Palamás!'
The world will echo his name!

Sound, trumpets! Thundering bells,
shake the land bodily, end to end!
Roar, bugles of war! Sacred
banners, unfurl in the wind!

On this coffin rests Greece! People,
raise your eyes and see her.
The temple is on fire, the sanctuary is burning,
and he is canopied with clouds of glory.

For above us, where the inexpressible pulse
of eternity flashes, at this hour,
Orpheus, Heraclitus, Aeschylus and Solomos
receive this holy, triumphant soul,

who built his work on deep foundations,
with godlike thought rooted in this earth;
and carry this thrice-blessed Iacchus aloft
to dance with the immortal gods.

Sound, trumpets! Thundering bells,
shake the land bodily, end to end!
Roar, Paean! Fearsome banners,
unfurl in the wind of Freedom!

Joseph Heller

Catch 22 (1961)

"There was only one catch and that was Catch-22, which
specified that a concern for one's safety in the face of dangers
that were real and immediate was the process of a rational
mind. Orr was crazy and could be grounded. All he had to do
was ask, and as soon as he did, he would no longer be crazy
and would have to fly more missions. Orr would be crazy to
fly more missions and sane if he didn't, but if he were sane if
he had to fly them. If he flew them he was crazy and didn't
have to; but if he didn't want to he was sane and had to."

J.R.R. Tolkein

The Two Towers (1954)

"War must be, while we defend our lives against a destroyer who would devour all; but I do not love the bright sword for its sharpness, nor the arrow for its swiftness, nor the warrior for his glory. I love only that which they defend."

Dr. Strangelove (1964)

The unhinged General Jack D. Ripper wanting to order a nuclear strike on the Russians:

"War is too important to be left to politicians. They have neither the time, the training, nor the inclination for strategic thought."

A Bridge Too Far (1977)

The story of the Allied attempt in WWII to break through German lines and relieve the forces holding Arnhem Bridge:

"Have you ever been liberated before?"
Lt. Colonel J.O.E. Vandeleur

"I got divorced twice. Does that count?"
Colonel Robert Stout

"It counts."
Lt. Colonel J.O.E. Vandeleur

Apocolypse Now (1979)

In the epic film about the Vietnam War, Lt Colonel Bill Kilgore commenting on his fondness for the incendiary napalm:

"I love the smell of napalm in the morning. You know, one time we had a hill bombed for 12 hours. When it was all over, I walked up. We didn't find one of 'em, not one stinkin' dink body. The smell, you know that gasoline smell, the whole hill. Smelled like … victory. Someday this war's gonna end…"

Saving Private Ryan

The 1998 film was set in Normandy in 1944 as a troop of US soldiers search for the last surviving brother of four servicemen.

"We're not here to do the decent thing, we here to follow f***ing orders."

LEST WE FORGET LAST WORDS

"It is foolish and wrong to mourn the men who died. Rather we should thank God that such men lived."

General Patton

Plato

Classical Greek philosopher (424–348BC)

"Only the dead have seen the end of war."

Hannibal

Carthaginian general (247–182BC)

"God has given to man no sharper spur to victory than contempt of death."

Julius Caesar

Describing in 47 BC how he conducted his brief campaign against Pharnaces II of Pontus in the city of Zela:

"Veni, vidi, vici"
(*"I came, I saw, I conquered"*)

Thomas Babington Macaulay, Lord Macaulay

From Macaulay's epic poem (1842) relating how Horatius defended Rome in 508BC from Lars Porsena, an Etruscan King.

Then out spake brave Horatius,
The Captain of the gate:
'To every man upon this earth
Death cometh soon or late.
And how can man die better
Than facing fearful odds,
For the ashes of his fathers,
And the temples of his Gods

Genghis Khan

Legendary warrior (1162 (approx) – 1227) and over 25 years founded the great Mongol Empire in Central Asia.'

"With Heaven's aid I have conquered for you a huge empire. But my life was too short to achieve conquest of the world."

Siward – Earl of Northumberland

In 1055 the great warrior was disappointed to discover he was dying of dysentery rather than nobly in battle as he would have expected:

"How shameful it is that I, who could not die in so many battles, should have been saved for the ignominious death of a cow! At least clothe me in my impenetrable breastplate, gird me with my sword, place my helmet on my head, my shield in my left hand, my gilded battle-axe in my right, that I, the bravest of soldiers may die like a soldier."

King Harold of England

Just before his untimely death at the Battle of Hastings (1066) which gave William of Normandy the English throne, King Harold had fought off a Viking invasion in a Battle at Stamford Bridge 200 miles to the North. This was led by his brother Tostig and Harold Hadraada of Norway, and when the Viking negotiations to claim a large part without a battle broke down, Harold was asked what he would actually give Hadraada. His reply was:

"Seven feet of English burial ground, or as much more that is needed – and he may be taller than other men."

Louis VI

King of the Franks (1108–1137)

"Better a thousand times to die with glory than to live without honour."

Admiral Lord Nelson

This was said by Nelson on the approach of the French Fleet, prior to the Battle of Trafalgar (1805) and just after he had sent out his famous "England expects…" signal:

"Now I can do no more. We must trust to the Great Disposer of all events and the justice of our cause. I thank God for this opportunity of doing my duty."

He was mortally wounded and his dying words include:

"Thank God I have done my duty."

Lieutenant-Colonel William Inglis

During the Battle of Albuera in 1811, at the height of the Peninsular war against the French, Lieutenant-Colonel William Inglis, the commanding officer of the 57th (West Middlesex) Regiment of Foot, was very badly wounded by grapeshot but refused to be removed from the battle. Despite the severity of his wounds he continued to exhort his regiment with these words:

"Die hard, 57th, die hard!"

The English line held against a superior enemy force and Inglis' words led to the 57th 's nickname – "The Die Hards" – and also their motto "Die Hard".

General John Sedgewick

American war of Independence – Battle of Spotsylvania 9 May 1864:

"Don't worry boys, They couldn't hit an elephant at this dist…"

At this moment, he fell dead – shot by Confederate sharpshooters about 500 metres away. He was the highest ranking Union casualty of the war.

Robert E. Lee

American Civil War commander of the Confederate Army of North Virginia:

"The education of a man is never completed until he dies."

"Get correct views of life, and learn to see the world in its true light. It will enable you to live pleasantly, to do good, and, when summoned away, to leave without regret."

William Tecumseh Sherman

Union general – American Civil War (1861-1865):

"I am tired and sick of war. Its glory is all moonshine. It is only those who have neither fired a shot nor heard the shrieks and groans of the wounded who cry aloud for blood, for vengeance, for desolation. War is hell."

Archduke Franz Ferdinand of Austria

The last words of the Franz Ferdinand, heir to the Austro-Hungarian throne, on his assassination in Sarajevo on 28th June 1914, and whose death was the catalyst that started World War I.

"It is nothing. It is nothing."

Brigadier General the Earl of Longford

Orders just before he died commanding 2nd Mounted Brigade – Gallipoli, August 1915

"Don't bother ducking, the men don't like it and it doesn't do any good."

Mustafa Kemal Atatürk

Atatürk was a division commander during the Battle of Gallipoli in 1915, and led the anti-Imperialist resistance that forced the withdrawal of the Allied forces. After the war, he erected a monument at Gallipoli, upon which was engraved the following words:

"Those heroes that shed their blood and lost their lives, you are now lying in the soil of a friendly country. Therefore, rest in peace. There is no difference between the Johnnies and the Mehmets to us where they lie side by side, now in this country of ours. You, the mothers who sent their sons from far away countries, wipe away your tears; your sons are now lying in our bosom, and are at peace. After having lost their lives on this land, they have become our sons as well."

Admiral Yamamoto

*Admiral Yamamoto helped to mastermind the Japanese Navy's
1941 surprise attack on the US Navy in Pearl Harbour and
which resulted in America joining World War II.
He commented with accurate foreboding:*

"In the first six months I will win victory after victory. But if
the war continues after that, I have no expectation of success. I
fear that all we have done is to awaken a sleeping giant and fill
him with a terrible resolve."

General Douglas MacArthur

*Douglas MacArthur was an American general (and also field
marshal of the Philippine army) who was Chief of Staff of the
United States Army during the 1930s.*

"They died hard, those savage men - like wounded wolves at
bay. They were filthy, and they were lousy, and they stunk.
And I loved them."

General George Patton

*American General who made his name successfully
commanding US troops in North Africa and Europe during
World War II*

"No bastard ever won a war by dying for his country. He won
it by making the other poor dumb bastard die for his country."

Mahatma Ghandi

Leader of Indian nationalism and non-violent civil disobedience until his assassination in 1948:

"I am prepared to die, but there is no cause for which I am prepared to kill."

Che Guevara

International Marxist revolutionary who was captured and executed in 1967

"I know you've come to kill me. Shoot, coward, you are only going to kill a man."

Just before he was executed by a Bolivian soldier Che was asked if he was thinking of his own mortality. He replied:

"No, I am thinking about the immortality of the revolution."

Ironically his immortality lives on through the commercial marketing of his image on T-shirts and posters.

Saddam Hussein

Vainglorious claim prior to the Iraq war in 2003:

"The Iraqi people are capable of fighting to the victorious end which God wants... The blood of our martyrs will burn you!"

Duke of Wellington

"My heart is broken by the terrible loss I have sustained in my old friends and companions and my poor soldiers. Believe me, nothing except a battle lost can be half so melancholy as a battle won."

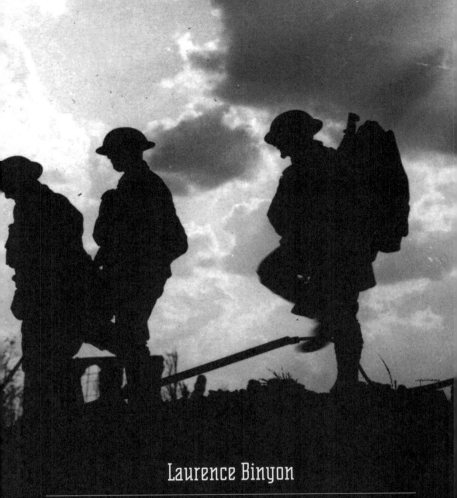

Laurence Binyon

*Poet, dramatist and scholar Binyon wrote this poem in 1914
on Pentire Cliffs in Cornwall in response to high number of
casualties already sustained early in World War I. The last two
verses are an integral part of Remembrance Day:*

"They went with songs to the battle, they were young.
  Straight of limb, true of eyes, steady and aglow.

They were staunch to the end against odds uncounted,
  They fell with their faces to the foe.

They shall grow not old, as we that are left grow old:
  Age shall not weary them, nor the years condemn.

At the going down of the sun and in the morning,
  We will remember them."